I Heard It Through the Grapevine

Selected Publications by Jeremy Reed

Poetry
Isthmus of Samuel Greenberg (1976)
Bleecker Street (1980)
By The Fisheries (1984)
Nero (1985)
Selected Poems (1987)
Engaging Form (1988)
Nineties (1990)
Red Haired Android (1992)
Kicks (1994)
Pop Stars, with Mick Rock (1995)
Sweet Sister Lyric (1996)
Saint Billie (2000)
Patron Saint of Eyeliner (2000)
Heartbreak Hotel (2002)
Duck and Sally Inside (2006)
Orange Sunshine (2006)
This Is How You Disappear (2007)
West End Survival Kit (2009)
Bona Drag (2009)
Black Russian: Out-takes from the Airmen's Club 1978-9 (2010)
Piccadilly Bongo (with Marc Almond) (2010)
Bona Vada (2011)
Whitehall Jackals (with Chris McCabe) (2013)
The Glamour Poet vs. Francis Bacon, Rent and Eyelinered Pussycat Dolls (2014)
Sooner or Later Frank (2014)

Novels
The Lipstick Boys (1984)
Blue Rock (1987)
Red Eclipse (1989)
Inhabiting Shadows (1990)
Isidore (1991)
When the Whip Comes Down (1992)
Chasing Black Rainbows (1994)
The Pleasure Chateau (1994)
Diamond Nebula (1995)
Red Hot Lipstick (1996)
Sister Midnight (1997)
Dorian (1998)
Boy Caesar (2004)
The Grid (2008)
Here Comes the Nice (2011)

I Heard It Through the Grapevine

—Asa Benveniste and Trigram Press—

JEREMY REED

WITH UNCOLLECTED WORK BY

ASA BENVENISTE

Shearsman Books

This edition published in the United Kingdom in 2016 by
Shearsman Books
50 Westons Hill Drive
Emersons Green
BRISTOL
BS16 7DF

Shearsman Books Ltd Registered Office
30–31 St. James Place, Mangotsfield, Bristol BS16 9JB
(this address not for correspondence)

ISBN 978-1-84861-463-5

ACKNOWLEDGEMENTS
The publisher would like to thank John Robinson of Joe DiMaggio Press for
permission to reprint *Edge* (1970) in its entirety, the editors of *Poltroon*
for permission to use the extract from *Asa Benveniste,*
Language Enemy Pursuit (1980), and Agneta Falk,
Asa's executor and luminous companion.

Contents

I

Heard

It

Through

the

Grapevine

For John Robinson, Mark Jackson and Tony Frazer
for continuing Asa's work.

The Man in Black

Asa Benveniste's poetry, a submerged cult to those in the know, takes as its resources a US-inflected tone and brokers an image-packed line as individual as any you'll get in the blue transitioning air-miles of seventies trans-Atlantic poetry.

Dressed in a black shirt, black jeans and black boots, thin as the Camel cigarette that was the natural extension of a hand signatured by foggy moonstones, intensely energised within a framework of quietly phrased cool, Asa first came into my life as a disaffected teenager, visiting me in Jersey with copies of his *AtoZ Formula*, Tom Raworth's *Big Green Day* and Nathaniel Tarn's *October*, as significant pointers opening a pathway into new poetry. Visiting Jersey to meet a potential backer for Trigram Press, and having read some of my early poetry that John Robinson's Joe Di Maggio Press had placed his way, Asa astonished me by requesting a book of mine for Trigram, something I felt unable to meet at the time, while beginning the process of regularly sending him poems and receiving enthused letters by way of return. My early, densely image-layered poems in which a charged impacted language compensated for imagined rather than real experience were largely the result of overdosing on Hart Crane. Crane as a boozed-up, Sophie Tucker and sailors-addicted gay maverick, who binged himself into writing state-altering hallucinated poetry in which language was often compressed to shattering, quickly became my prototype for writing urban poems saturated in marine colours and imagery. Asa, who shared Crane's brand choice of Cutty Sark whisky, was also an admirer of Hart's ability to torch-up language right to the fractional edge of the possible.

From that first grey sea-foggy day that he broke into my life Asa has been consistently my poetic avatar, my ideal of the poet as the thin man burning intense energies like a verbal contrail. Submerged in, and often concealed behind, the poets he published, initially printing the books letterpress, assisted by his stepson Paul Vaughan at the Trigram base, 148 King's Cross Road, London WC1, Asa masked his own identity as a poet behind his recognition as one of the most innovative publishers of the late sixties – together with Cape Goliard and Fulcrum Press. While Asa to my mind always wrote significantly ahead of his contemporaries, he lacked all incentive to go public, preferring instead to remain underground, treating the process of writing as something concealed, like laundering cash in a cellar.

Asa's poetry involves the real work of making language physical, something he was acutely aware of as a printer. You can feel the textural quality of his words, the chunky solidity of how they sit on the page occupying typographic space. A typical Benveniste poem, with its disruptively fractured narrative, takes as its starting point a domestic moment, often a randomised visual image that in turn leads directly to another by way of association. Usually shared with a few interested friends, or placed in small magazines, Asa kept his poems back as work-in-progress: a neglected, because there was no one to find it, and carefully maintained secret. And because of his cutting-edge reputation as a publisher with Trigram Press he tended to be invariably the recipient of other's people's solicited or unsolicited poems – poets wanted his attention – and didn't give him theirs. Asa tended to work in secret, and during the years I visited him at 22 Leverton Street, the open-plan conversion he occupied in London's Kentish Town, he was writing and rarely showing, breaking silence only with the group of poems published in *Dense Lens* (1975) and arguably with his best book *Edge* (1975), one permeated by a Chinese aesthetic, published by John Robinson's Joe Di Maggio Press, with John mimeographing the stapled A4 book in his bedroom at 23 Fairmead Road and Pip Benveniste supplying the out-of-focus photo of Asa, silkscreened on the front cover. *Edge*, largely published to be given away to friends and sold at outlets like Compendium, was published in an edition of 350 copies, with Asa characteristically and self-deprecatingly telling John to keep most of the copies submerged in his back room. And of course that's how most significant non-mainstream poetry circulates – by a process of filtering copies to sympathetic friends.

Asa's beginnings in poetry, the densely oblique *Poems of the Mouth* (1966) and *The AtoZ Formula* (1969), both published by Trigram, were essentially hermetic shape-shifting language games with Kabbala and the *I Ching* as their image resources, and the poet working with language as a sort of code-breaking process on the secrets it both conceals and reveals about reality. Asa in fact omitted both books from his Selected Poems, *Throw Out the Life Line Lay Out the Corse: Poems 1965-1985*, substituting his early kabbalistic preoccupations with the marginally more accessible *The Alchemical Cupboard*, as representative of the mystic soup he was linguistically cooking in the sixties. Asa regarded most post-1950s mainstream British poetry as obdurately resistant to US experimentation via Black Mountain and the O'Hara/Ashbery bouncy New York influence vitally energising subcultures like pop, sex, drugs, and the whole urban streetwise dynamic that was the signposting of modern life, and the breaking-up of formal poetics into edgier reconfigured patterns.

In London Asa largely lived on plain yoghurts, cheese and biscuits, brutally aromatic black Turkish coffee, purchasing the beans from a store on South Moulton Street, periodic pizza forays, whiskey, sunrise-red bloody marys, red wine and American toasted cigarettes like softpack non-filter Lucky Strike and Camel. A poet's individual choice of nutrition and stimulants is a key factor affecting the protein syntheses and neural gateways into the work, and Asa's emphasis on food was ascetically minimal, and on booze, fags and joints optimal. When he wasn't in London he got away to his flatland village hideaway, Blue Tile House in Fakenham, Norfolk, where I visited him one colour-drenched October, and where his enmity with Pip was visible in their frozen relations, even apparent to a stranger. Asa appeared cut-off, detached and morosely preoccupied, with his own constant sense of inner disquiet. His periodic getaways only served to enhance his mystique, as though the man in black needed occult rehabilitation before re-immersing himself in big city affairs. What he had though was an unparalleled facility for design, fonts, the visually quirky and the accidental risk that became a book's personality and which so distinguished him as top of the game as a brilliant, one-off, maverick publisher. Asa was spontaneous in his likes and accepted Paul Gogarty's *Snap Box* (1972), a small rectangular book printed on blue paper and brimming with fragmented pop hooks, within hours of the poet randomly hand-delivering the manuscript to Asa in person. There was no systemised formula to Trigram Press, Asa picked up what he published on his own quirky crypto-allusive radar.

I come back again to language, and how for Asa its process as the building blocks of imagery in a poem, were engineered to open up big interactive space-times through associated inner states, as the poem's rich cultural signposting.

> What can he do with all that dust?
> there are so many American poets
> (I mean pilots) just waiting
> on the back of tomorrow's tortoise
> in jasmine corridors who question
> after question

There's so much connotative space and time-travel in Asa's poetry, and in *Language: Enemy, Pursuit* (1980) he tells us in a rare confessional admission that his qualifiers for a poem are 'it must have no beginning or conclusion. If it's about anything it must be language. That's the only kind of poem that will keep its divinity. It must have 600,000 meanings and in the end be meaningless.' Asa's poetic signifiers, coming in part from a long immersion in the Torah place him radically outside contemporary mainstream poets programmed in the belief that a poem must find an apparent resolution to its inception. Asa on the contrary deals possibilities that aren't solutions but alternative readings to his theme, rather in the way that Pound's *Cantos* don't subscribe to anything but their own personalised content.

I've been a lifelong AB addict, reading his poems often on a daily basis, not only for the visually compelling imagery they throw up, but for their instantly refreshing sense of making poetry new and staying that way. There are so many ways of reading a Benveniste poem, that yes in his signifying terms, you have 600,000 alternative pathways as access. There's nothing difficult about Asa's poetry, not in the way of Louis Zukofsky's crunched linguistics or J.H. Prynne's emotionless postmodernism, or for that matter *down*, although he often appeared that; rather, there's an exhilarating upward curve to the writing, working language into the domestic zone in which we mostly live. It's significant that when Asa gave up printing Trigram Press books in 1974, largely for health reasons and the poisoning he periodically experienced on account of the toxicity of working with metals – having instead to job the work out and meticulously oversee design – the nature of his poetry turned more lyrical, as though liberated from the exacting self-conscious process of setting print he was personally freed into a less constrained medium. The work collected in *Pommes Poems* (1988) being amongst the most beautiful he achieved in letting go that little extra into sustained lyric focus. Printing, the hard physical graft of it wore Asa out and in *Language: Enemy, Pursuit* he speaks forcibly of his shattering. 'Vile metal: the worst, intractable element for anyone, a poet most of all, to deal with every day of his life. I recognise the metal men now, the calipers men, when I pass them in the street. They have burn marks on their skin, singed hair, their eyes opaque, black, they've lost the ability to listen. Their hands are like cities, one has to walk around them as one would walk around mangled cars, and I surrendered to those razor sharp edges too long.'

Asa's reasons for writing poetry were equally integrated into his frustrations in realising that poetry is largely impotent to change reality, even if its expression creates the illusion that it can and will alter the social context given time. All good writing occupies the present that is of course the future. To stay in poetry you need to accept you're going nowhere but making it happen in the real-time exciting specifics of the journey. It's a difficult one to take on, as the pursuit implies an edgy mental alienation and in Asa's case dejection, heavy drinking, marital discord – Pip would complain that nothing alleviated his disparaged sense of occupying the edge – and Asa invariably stayed there as the state he best knew. His later poems, written after crawling out of the exploded debris of his marriage to Pip and relocating with his new partner Agneta Falk to Hebden Bridge in Yorkshire, are altogether more celebratory in tone and winning in their lyrically nuanced windows.

> The sky lowers itself to my book
> and your reading of it as blue,
> Materia prima, are, as if the touch
> was perfectly defined, the terminal
> occurrence when ceiling plaster floated
> along the surface of crepes normandes
> steeped in biting calvados. I thought of you
> on the channel boat, speculating on your arrival
> at Honfleur to research Boudin mysteries,
> such light, the blue wind bleaching shingle
> to an almost undefinable white.

This is as good as you'll get optimal blue lyricism, and all of Pommes Poems constitutes a progressive breakthrough in spontaneity, as though Asa was better committed to the poem's autonomous momentum, rather than its fractured splintering. Asa worked characteristically slowly, building the image connectivity of each poem like the stages of a clinical drugs trial, his last poems accumulating in a dull grey portfolio, lacking previous publication in small magazines and ultimately designed to outstrip his body and go on speaking for the last stages of his life. Liver-damaged and acutely undermined by diabetes brought on by heavy drinking, he worked the line for the first time against real rather than imagined death. In his letters to me at the time he spoke of being unable to give up drinking red wine, even after the amputation of his left leg due to diabetes-related gangrene; and of his empathetic association with Arthur Rimbaud who, on returning from Aden to the Hôpital de la Conception, in Marseilles, on 20 May 1891, and diagnosed with aggressive bone cancer, became an amputee with a wooden leg on 27 May, before dying of complications on November 10 of the same year. The near-death crisis and irreversible loss of a leg drove Asa forward, as though writing which had once been a reluctant concession on his part to liberate the poem onto the page was now a charged necessity. Driven in on himself and facing his mutilated body there was no other option. The poems collected in *Invisible Ink* (1989), are amongst the most incisively personal he wrote, without ever abandoning his idiosyncratic formula of placing language in the frontline of poetic investigation. And of course the figure of Arthur Rimbaud remains the subtext spook to Asa's difficult rehabilitation to accepting his irreparably altered body.

It rubs away keening flesh
to the thinnest blade of shin
and knee, and are my weapons,
my cutting pen on paper
I cannot reach for
without invoking the surgeon's
pulsing blade and rasp,
who has amputated his own
heart, as Rimbaud described,
citing my own loving act.
Loving? Can it be true?

In 'Falling' Asa refers to 'the vulnerable drag on my leg/ blood falling like pollenous sap through the bandages' as he attempted to orientate to having a stump instead of a functional leg. His last small collection has amputation as its central focus, co-opting Rimbaud in as an underwritten spook to poems that don't emotionally compensate for harrowing physical loss and living with it. In 'Cut' Asa establishes the verb as an incision as much applied to language as to flesh.

It has never been so important to cut
into dreams the right words,
like an insane collage where the scalpel
is language expunged by sight loss
and often has no connection with acts

that pass for theatre: a marble head,
a lion's bleeding mouth, the dawn black
with cross-hatchings incised on steel.

In what was his last letter to me from 68 Bridge Lanes, Hebden Bridge, dated mid-November 1989, Asa spoke of his total inactivity, mentally and physically, almost the abandonment of his art, concurrent with his approaching death in April 1990. 'Your book came yesterday, and I've begun to read it. Very exciting. Bless you for writing it and for sending it to me. I don't know why I haven't written sooner, except to say that I haven't written anything in the past two months, even letters piling up on my desk like a dust storm. I am facing the black screen. Aggie keeps telling me to work, work, and if only I had your facility to make books dance. I know I must, but I can't bear it. I listen to the radio occasionally, see whoever comes to my room, otherwise I stare at the fire when it's on and remember. Sleep catches me at odd moments during the day, and at night when I need it it eludes me. I can't do anything except wait for it to pass. It's terrible as you know, as you can guess.'

Uncomplaining, Asa who'd always had a dread of physical illness, invariably imagining covert symptoms accreting undercover in his body without becoming physicalised, was now faced with what he called the black screen that didn't even lend itself to his facility with language. His move to Yorkshire, where he partly ran a second-hand bookshop, had removed him from his London friends, and geographical isolation after big city busyness only enhanced his sense of alienation. There's something about the stupendous momentum of London's energies that locks you into capital affairs, and my hectic day to day agenda of writing and social activities prevented me seeing Asa after he left London, despite repeated intentions to do so, as it did our mutual friend John Robinson, who also remained constrained by work in town, despite our periodically raised joint plans to drive to Hebden Bridge together.

On 15 April 1990 I received a short note in Aggie's hand telling me "Asa died Friday night. I will tell you later why and how, but for now I find it difficult to speak. I'm in such pain that I can barely hold this pen. You must forgive me for not writing more at this moment. I will let you know when he is going to be buried. Perhaps you would like to read something?" Asa's house on Leverton Street outlives him in London's continuously reconstructed upmarket present in which all central property is zoned into high-end, and going back there I'm left to imagine Asa as residual identity, a sort of post-human download substituting for the thin figure in a charcoal crew neck lambswool jumper and dark blue jeans, dragging intensely on a Marlboro Lite's loopy blue smoke, as he threw shapes with his quietly inflected voice. I remember his enthusiasm on discovering the Canadian language poet Christopher Dewdney's seminal collections, *A Palaeozoic Geology of London, Ontario* (1973), and *Fovea Centralis* (1975), and recommending them to me, and the delight he took in Barry MacSweeney's extravagantly phrased and dope-hallucinated *Six Odes*, in the typographical outlay of a randomly chanced-on ad in a magazine, or whatever impacted visually on his retina and could be used as a detail in his acutely individual sense of book design for Trigram Press.

Asa's sympathetic understanding of life, and how one's inner direction was so often contrary to systems opposing the individual, made him a deeply valued friend. In my case he got me away from the suffocating cultural restrictions of my birthplace, Jersey C.I, to registering as an undergraduate at Essex University, studying American Literature, with an emphasis on Black Mountain poetry, as seminal to my development as a poet. Asa's one visit to Jersey and his apprehension over my simply not belonging there precipitated my coming to live in London and finding acceptance amongst my chosen milieu, as well as explosively available highways for my writing. If you were in trouble he'd sit with you and talk aspects of problems, and he'd be in them too, only he was trying to show you possible ways through or out the tunnel. If his own poetic preoccupations often focused on the correlation between language and death, 'Even in death it's language first,' then counterpointing the downward pull of gravity was a sensual aesthetic that correspondingly eroticised the poem into figurative expression. He taught all of us who were Trigram poets that the image came first as the poem's drive-unit, and that a poem without polyvalent imagery is like a pop song without a hook, it doesn't stick.

Even today I test what I write against his imagined approval or disapproval. If it isn't weird enough then push it out further to the edge and saturate the image. Always write like you're inventing tomorrow, that's my reason for doing poetry, unlike mainstream poets who are frozen into a largely redundant past.

That Asa's poems haven't to date been assembled into a *Collected*, as a rich comprehensive overview of his life's work, is a serious omission, given that most of his contemporaries have been better rewarded. I imagine, given his incurable self-deprecation, that that's what he would have expected, the indomitable exclusion factor that inexplicably counts some poets in and others out. There's no poet I read so often and with such personal gain as Asa Benveniste, and partly because a single poem of his opens out into a rich library of personal associations that collapse the distance between text and reader, and in the literal sense of the word, fascinate by their not being like anyone else's poetry. Asa's advice to me right from the start was US influence, in other words bypass the British modality of reported social realism and focus on everything that isn't usually acceptable subject matter for poetry – what's right in front of you and what you shouldn't be doing at the time, but admit to.

The dossiers that make up this interactive book, my poems about Asa and anecdotal commentaries on him and his work, together with a selection of his 1970s poetry only available in small press booklets is aimed at some sort of restorative faculty for a poet waiting to surprise readers by his overextended absence.

Odd As You Do
Poems About Asa

Colour Theory

Six extravagant peach-yellow roses
like masculinity that's soft
imploded into self-review
like Asa's ontological zero
Colour Theory laid flat on the table
immaculate desert design
white space compensates for typography
a moonscape situating words
in ink that's black as opium paste
language always arriving from the left
and tracking right over
the central reservation, getting there
as imaginative mobility –
the end an underground car park's
shoot out potentialities.
It seems so long ago today
so yesterday overtakes it
language like a crunchy sandwich
popped with verbal salad
always written in the present
and that afternoon six floppy yellow roses
glassed on the pine table at Leverton Street
Colour Theory arrived from the printer
my copy signed in black AB
the signature transmitting a paper heartbeat.

Black

A black shirt
black as absorbent
differential, carpaint black
as Chinese hair
the Trigram avatar
in black – white paper
the contrast Old Turkey,
Abbey Mills, names like whiskey brands
to spatialize a font,
black jeans a colour split
into no-colour variant
always back to black
as dominant, you said to me –
'even in death it's language first'
like the other side of poetry
we meet again as diagram
or violet tinted
hologram, a book you'd say's
only physical consolidation
you've moved your hand
west-east meridian
getting there by non-linear
space-hops – and Asa's black coffee
mixed Turkey like black pigment in a cup.

Layout

You'd walk in open plan, toned walnut floor,
room arrangement like book design
spatialized as one-to-two resonance,
white furniture, white blocks for books,
ultramarine sofa, pine desk
light as a surf board, I Ching open
presenting image – a trigram
black ink brushstroke like a boxy hairdo,
a Leonard Cohen poster on the wall,
clean poetry clinic, language menu
criterion for acceptance: –
'only the image counts: one perception
leads directly to another' – modern
the only option, like Leverton Street,
Cutty Sark, Maker's Mark and J&B
poured out as angled dollops, ropy, neat,
liberating vision into cool line,
mid-life, mid-week, stepping out to the street
as best spontaneous take on reality.

Drink

A shot like a hot handgun
blocky with Lego building bricks
of clunky ice, Absolut, Smirnoff
dosed red as a Martian landscape,
sherry, mint, horse radish,
the in-glass kicky boosters
for the ultimately disillusioned
dejected melancholic –
you don't need to cross a desert
the world's contained in a yard,
scotch, bourbon and other snifters,
Wild Turkey, Jack Daniels, Teachers,
the sting's like whiskey maths
an Einstein graffiti Sanskrit
complicating the senses.
Asa didn't do fingers
only over-poured approximate measures
the glass competing with the bottle
and always so far ahead
with no hangover frontier
drizzling an aching stop
like it takes 20 minutes
email travel from Mars to Earth,
same time it takes booze to kick in
to altering chemical level
a glow like a whiskey mixer
come up as a spinning orange aura.

Blue Tile House

A Fakenham Norfolk retreat,
no signposting, flatland prairies,
a chill out with fog at a gradient
like a grainy psychedelic
halo, you couldn't remember the way
and a red and gold pagoda
lumped in a field was a pub
with directionless rural dialect
like talking of off-world planets
mining helium-3 on the moon
but it was only the next village,
Pip in the house, your estranged
disinterested co-dependent
independently motivated (wife)
there was only one room held focus
in a stone/wood American plan
with a fire rearranging patterns
all the rest was empty cold space
like your redundant marriage
left in the fridge for years:
and I stayed up half the night writing
the Valium didn't work
thinking of who and what I'd done
to make poetry my best friend
with your enthused validation
and the fog split open like a peach
6 a.m. with the scarlet rising sun.

Odd As You Do

As hobbyist I collect Trigram Press,
fetish paper smell, back matter colophon,
words set like black fuck-me pumps
with affirmative five-inch heels
A Word In Your Season or the blowjob
in its industrial silver portfolio
or simultaneous with his suicide
B.S. Johnson's Poems Two
the mood tougher than kicking in a door.
There's Big Green Day with its Jim Dine jacket
green printed red as state-altering trick.
Collecting's like a gantried rocket
with a twenty-year hangover
pointing nose up at a curved cloudy sky
that solitary. The man who made these books
was built of language, his dejections blue
as a windowless cellar's indigo,
his method breaking every printer's rule
to outdetail detail. He comes back at me,
aluminium jumper, dusty blue jeans,
no interest in distributing titles
only doing specials. One blueberry yoghurt a day,
40 Camel cigarettes – the word raised
on grained paper – every book a metaphor
to Americanise Brit poetry,
Leverton Street outside and Asa's door
of course he opened it with a gold key.

B.S.

Johnson.
Kentish Town truculent
maverick elephant
his solo fiction surgery
scrambling linear
into randomised asymmetric chance
a bottle of Famous Grouse
his signposting instructor
Aren't You Aren't You Aren't You
Far Too Young To Be Writing Your Memoirs
it's timing good as Sinatra's
instructively spacing a phrase
it's the poet in him rocks
my metabolic juices
Poems and Poems 2
tight as a panic attack
and hands on like scooping shingle
on a Thames beach for lucked on gold.
It's his imagery slices
into my visual frames
rude attitude infecting
everything he did as loner
irascible liver fatty
loser, giving words a helium lift,
slashing his wrists in the saturated colour bath
like Beaujolais – the preconceived edit
a half bottle of brandy
for whoever found him dead.
Death
Post-human blank, no physicals,
there's death online if you click mirage men
and go extraterrestrial
space-hop.
It's one way like a Mars mission
looking to source oxygen/hydrogen
convertible to raw rocket fuel,

no re-entry as same individual.
For years I packaged my death wish at Kentish Town,
shared it with Asa in his open-plan
aspecting imaginative flightpaths
without radar. 22 Leverton Street,
my death academy, vampish Turkish coffee
flavouring ambience, like warm jeans pulled
out of the planet-spinning dryer.
If I returned before I died, would it
be older, younger or no-age?
Asa's discovered what I don't know yet,
admissions, deciding today
if my mother's coffin should be oak veneer
or eco-friendly wicker, sitting out
the cloud-choked June afternoon, grey on grey,
hoping as always for a messenger.

AtoZ

Initialized at first reading
into phrases dusting my breath
26 choices permutations
I learnt to American read
words as spatial geographies
a violet storm in my window
shattering glitzy sparkles
me cornered by alienation
in aqua Jersey CI
islanded by anxiety
and the green sea's exclusion zone
listening to Leonard Cohen's down
in the bottom depression
like a pitted avocado stone
and something in Asa's lines
lifting me out of insularity
into space as inclusion
at a centimetre a time
advance, oh I used to sing
'when I'm dead and gone'
before I'd started, moody on beaches
where the sea left blue sea jewels
in rock pools – and I was done
outed into the turbulent sky
nose cone into an equivocal future
in a city where every stranger
encountered became a story
I keep on daily adding to mine.

Archaeologist of Morning

Mine's the Cape Goliard block
ISBN 206 61880
designed and printed unimpeachably
as a frenched low-skirted Cadillac
by Barry Hall as gateways-svengali
to letting US Black Mountain in
like an illegal substance
and its physical work like a summit
achieved at Fairhazel Gardens
a book that palpably weighs in
like Charles Olson 6'7"
calorific with booze as directive
using words like spot-gold index
syllables by organic ounce
and published posthumously
November 1970
the big man's scattered poems collected
without him being there
in his black and white Converse All Star,
royal blue lettering on the jacket
off-white nude-coloured paper
a customised monument
to a lifetime working humane lines
spatialized into a Gloucester atlas
that touching the font seems permanent.

Casuals

At Uni thought I'd live for ever
like a rockit jockey tracking
extraterrestrial trade routes
or as we imagined Bowie
as unstoppable looks imperator

coke as his rocky avatar
like granulated diamonds
mined by the senses for reward.
At Wivenhoe the river scrolled
angel-fish blue into regolith grey

as portable science lab colours.
Our Black Mountain tutor was so laid back
he seemed focused on cloud spotting
formations like purple neon
tapioca, taught us Olson

like ideas as helium.
Get a good poem you crunch
China in your hand, like a Kitkat bite
that's optimal choc and wafer.
Mostly we all stayed out to lunch.

Bowie's got a stent in his arteries
as payback, and I've lost it all
from lack of compromise, still read Olson,
recall the docks at Wivenhoe, no ships,
the orange cabined cranes dysfunctional.

Houseboat Days Remix

Altered state I got from John Ashbery
like hacking a plant hallucinogen
the light was different first time I read
less carbon dump with a pineapple twist
my neurons criss-crossing in 3D
like information exchanged in the cosmos.
Read what I picked up sunglassed by the sea
hazy green John Smedley wool V
moon-shaped hole left sleeve (got it cheap)
everything modern like I keep today
(molecules can't exist outside 3D)
the idea of myself interrupting
what was – I pick it up again the phrase
I'm looking for as post-immediacy.

Writing Don't Reach No-one

It's like in-flight food for Mars astronauts
{poetry} weirdo dialect,
vegetable sushi, jambalaya, pelmeni,
tested on northern slopes of Mauna Loa
(this is gene-free Soho poem)
like language bounced off the moon
the intersection of Frith and Old Compton Street
comes in as physical geography
street signs at a wraparound L
I've only got one avatar Asa
I live most days inside his poetry's
disruptive time-slips Chinese plum blossom
exploding from his imagery I mean
it's like that poets picked up by readers
as a shared secret and it still goes on.

This is English Poem

Cucumber crunchy paper
binder's glue whiffy as car upholstery
semi-aniline Nero Ade
(black) (black) (black)
like *lao gan ma* chilli black bean sauce
this is English poem (Asa's phrase)
Guangdong lapi chilled silk noodles
picked over in Kentish Town
where Asa's Botulism imprint
(botulism: L. botulus sausage + ism)
pointing up mainstream bacterial poetry
got launched from conversational aside
northeastern and Sichuan styles
like green and orange endpapers
as colour sumptuous invitation
to meet the margins inside, white space white
to the edge, like this is English poem
just like white Chinese chrysanthemum
reviewed once and left for ever
composed so strategically in autumn
it's exact like a footnote to Li Po
drunk and stoned on a boat on the river

Seventies

One acid microdot spatialized time,
I saw you Kevin through grey foggy arcs
like a prism of ruby laser light
molecularised hallucinogens
turning intelligence orange
as heartbeat to our reactive valley
(dense oaks with Portobello mushroom tops)
so green they looked like steamed spinach.
We lacked purchase on the decade we lived
as passport photo living it right in.
Goat's Head Soup as soundtrack, who remembers
'Coming Down Again, 'a drug drop
through lysergic pathways. Chased it all the day
elusive psychic memos, drug traces
like psychoactive architecture.
We got lost in knotty woods – you'd play spook
I'd follow off-script and sit down to view
a purple heartbeat pulsing in the fog.
Seventies, chased into a corridor
that de-realised like the house we found
as torched ruin, and kept coming back to,
a gutted piano, burnt books in tall weeds
a fire-cracked mirage emitting no sound.

Air (fucked) Quality

Got red Saharan dust smudged into smog
(Rimbaud crossed the desert in army boots
a street tough kicking Arab ass).
PM 2.5 particles, PM 10,
black diesel, nitrogen dioxide
101 ppb – the word evolves
as metabolised oxygen, its weight
constructed durability
zero mass like galactically sourced light
adjectival in red, blue, green, orange,
I'd prefer spontaneous telepathy
at nerve propagation speeds, speed-freak speed
chooser and chosen poetry, you know
the subject's a step-change behind
practitioners, and today red sunrise
is shaped like a yellow TV screen
over Canary Wharf, a foggy dub
on crane mobility – their dipping arms
slow as a heroin geography.

Sending Poetry

It's like drug efficacity
managing words for time release,
compacted, multitasking, targeted,
like building chunks of oil pipeline
from Blackpool or Oklahoma

think global – fuck with poetry
like getting a T-shirt slogan
hot pink with a graffiti font
an urban tag – Moon War 1 Survivor
and soon they'll war on the dusty plateau

territorialising regolith.
And miso soup – post-modern bulletin
to health, you need chopped spring onions
to tip the taste buds, I get mine
Wholefood on Soho's Brewer Street

to do stuff for immune. The thoughts you shared
were like an archipelago
of floating Lego, neural puffs
cut into diamond shapes, purples and blues
the cyan seen out of a plane.

Your old pop-up toaster's nail varnish red
for slinging multi-seed, a gunslinger,
our 8 a.m. module. It's on the map
the place this poem goes – I send it there:
the orbit's your guess Mars or Europa.

Habit

All my life 2 or 3
poems a day unstoppable
imaginative dependency
on state-altered imagery
like a space programme
worked in microgravity
or my parallel habit
Valium 10mgs
gotta have it, it can't be
diff to my neurology
hallucinated amygdala
damaged almond-shaped brain car park
torched-up like a Ferrari
at propulsive getaway.
Never failed me, got it right
from a dodgy deviant start
addiction to every day
weird as my reality
poetry as UFO
sightings – do you ever hear me
in book saturation no
got no credibility
outlaw to the whole quango
hate me for originality
writing on bank notes sometimes
to optimise immediacy
on a skinny knee in Leicester Square
do me in eventually.

'The trouble is the English are hung up on Larkin. Larkin was a poet of minute ambitions and carried them out exquisitely. But he really isn't a very important poet and right now he exercises a terrible influence on English poetry because if you admire somebody like that so much it means you're not going to be aiming very high.'

—Thom Gunn

Statement from Trigram 1969 catalogue

Trigram books are designed and printed in London by Asa Benveniste and Paul Vaughan on their own presses: a Glockner automatic cylinder and a Sericol screen print table. On the presumption that no one else can do the books as well as they. The press was started in 1965, and the intention was, and still is, to publish and print the most significant poetry/art being produced at this time, in a style that would clarify and illuminate the meaning of the text/image.

Four years later a clear editorial policy emerges. The writers and artists whose books have been published under the Trigram imprint appear to work in acute conditions of exile, living and thinking on the edges of society, some outside their own countries, others within, hallucinated by a series of mental doorways. In common, they have striven for an individual voice that in any circumstance has to be heard. No artist can do more or should do any less than that.

Language: Enemy, Pursuit

by

Asa Benveniste

You cut until you're down to three lights on the page, something as close to the truth as 'God the Word.' Not immediately enlightening except for the awareness that what one is heading for is silence. Language as an absurdity. Language as a means of suicide (Aragon). Suicide as a response to the absurd (Camus), caught again in the rigid limitations of moribund syntax. Artaud's screaming anathemata, Valery's twenty-year retirement, the dust of Dada and also, greatly, that Irish poet who abandoned the concise tracery of single-string plucking in order to write a block of allusive language as a commemoration to the death of itself, sidereal to that cortege which passes through everything we write. The gravedigger being the machinery we've evolved over the last 500 years to make the whole process of knowledgeable flight perpetrate the delusion of permanency. How can it be permanent? As law it does not survive dispute. As a precept it has about as much ability to withdraw from the disparities of dialectical confusion as water passing from earth to stem to leaves to flowers. Logical, causal, illusory pronunciations against the black exile of poem which in the beginning is bound to fail. I don't really want to be here. Every other word is enough to make the one preceding it lose its meaningfulness one third of a second after it's gone past.

In the fifteen years Trigram has been going I've become blinded by paper, the white, the black, the astrolabe of letters following so often the corrugation of pits, black within valleys of white, 'black fire on white fire' (Nahmanides), until, if one works on it over and over, one is left only with abrasions and light making its own apparencies. The most effective way of ruining good paper is to write on it (Johnson). Printing on it is more effective, like setting a match to the edges, flame working inward toward the centre. Now I spend a great deal of time just feeling the rectangularity of these constructs. Opening them in a ritual of ablution. One word is enough. Take it, use it on its own, you're left with he feeling that you have made statement out of nothing.

Already these words abominate me. I have only a small part in their construction, minor pitiable carrion useful only in drawing attention to them by my brain-damaged alienation from their shapely world. They are in being before I came on to the set, and they ignore me because at the same time that I consider myself obliquely responsible for their progression from one structure to another they have already made the transition. They are there, I camp follow, useful only in keeping out cross-traffic to make the sequentials easier. If it's meaningless they are still meaningful, if I am meaningful they are hardly likely to subsume it. It's always been a manoeuvre of mastery, and we have all of us, not just some of us, always lost. 'Thoth, the mind and tongue of Ra, the Word-god, through whose utterance all things come into material being.' I/you am/are not Thoth. I don't mention this interpretive myth as a form of prayer; only to remind myself that whereas the material has to wait for its utterance we are crippled by a power of speech so close to useless (word language, that is) we're left with only two or three ways to rise beyond it, most of them inadequate before the mysteries.

This is the exilic condition. We use a great deal of our time, when we can force ourselves to it, sharpening pencils, glancing off keys with a stiff brush, changing ribbons, imposition, measuring the distances between bolts and type on the page, head, tail, fore-edge, making certain the signatures follow each other accurately, disposition of face to content, and most importantly that the white spaces around it all provide a contemplative arena before the plunge into chaos. That the binding doesn't crack, that the open book lies flat on the table and that the pages turn easily in readable breath. Ritual fire, spinal fire, the printing press, so fierce banging away at such thin, inflammable material it's almost impossible to understand the way words are encapsulated so tidily, or is that an illusion also?

About a year after I started printing I dreamt about a box containing a depiction of the god of metal, Egyptian, flat, made of lead, lying in a small wooden coffin. The rite consisted of having to cut off part of my neck downward, as though it were roast beef. 'I feed on my own substance and do not renew myself' (Nerval). The left side, with my left hand. The word 'anoxia' was inscribed on the lid. Later that night I had a long dream about the killing of one of my sons, Paul, who worked with me at the press. He was about to be hung for murder. I stayed with him over a period of days. I escorted him, he was wearing a cowboy hat, to the place where he was to die, together with the body of the dead infant queen with whom he was to be buried, as she was the only other child in the country who had been hung before.

Gematria: a fierce confrontation with word, one of the best ways to barricade oneself against the confused inlay. Linguistics is not language. Communication is the last word to use to describe its purpose. Though to every poet, as to every Kabbalist, there must be more to those words than their beauty. That their meaninglessness itself is part of the divine (linguistic) fabric. In the end, at the start, early Kabbalists believed that the whole of the Torah consisted of one word only, though each of the letters had seventy aspects, and the Torah as a whole had 600,000 meanings, on four levels of interpretation, all leading to the profoundest meaning which was 'meaningless,' which was not open to understanding but was only itself.

And is that true of poetry? One thing it cannot be: story. It must not be based on experience, one of the forms of paralysis (Satie). It cannot be descriptive. It cannot be about love. It cannot be about hate. It cannot contain specific meaning. It must avoid sensuality. It must not be capable of restatement in another manner. It must not be allegorical. It cannot be translatable into a foreign language. It must be language. That's the only kind of poem that will keep its divinity. It must have 600,000 meanings and in the end be 'meaningless.'

I have never succeeded in printing a book that did not contain an error somewhere, no matter how carefully I prepared for the work. Rabbi Meir relates: 'when I went to Rabbi Ishmael he asked me: ' My son, be careful in your work, for it is the work of God; if you omit a single letter, or write a letter too many, you will destroy the world...'

Madness. The last book for which I was responsible, Zukofsky's *A 22 & 23*, one of the most textually difficult books the press has published, reached its final state, even after three gruelling, enlightening seasons of proof-reading and layout, with eight literals, (for each of the trigrams?). Zen errors perhaps, though for Zukofsky's state it saddened me. He was ill, looked forward to our edition and then I think, from a polite, firm note I had, was appalled at the inaccuracies in his tight, dense syntactical discoveries. I'm told he has died, but in England that's hardly the stuff of mawkish journalism, so I can't be sure. Is it true? Later, a small passage I found in the poem: 'A beast/ in a dream warns/ not to kill in all languages' in any language... but itself? Death?

Vile metal: the worst, intractable element for anyone, a poet most of all, to deal with every day of his life. I recognise the metal men now, the calipers men, when I pass them in the street. They have burn marks on their skin, singed hair, their eyes opaque, black, they've lost the ability to listen. Their hands are like cities, one has to walk around them as one would walk around mangled cars, and I surrendered to those razor sharp edges too long. Not languorously, like a Provençal dame looking at the poplared horizon for her armoured love to ride in. But hard, fighting fire with poem. The arrangements upon which I exercised an allusive geometry intuitively, non-informatively ('Truth is not true' – Queasy Malone), as close to the inner shell (the Torah as a nut) as I could penetrate, hoping that by containing idealised typography, colour, weight, space, perfected sheets, all the doorways, I might then do something acceptable about returning sparks to replenish earth, or wherever they spring from. And I did in one or two, three instances perhaps; that seemed to me enough. The rest of it lay too much on the surface, minor reflections of the sun, comely, conclusive in the best sense, my hand poisoned by antimony, head needling light or booze...oh, it's not that much of a Greek drama. I was just a rotten printer. It was beginning to ruin any pleasure I might derive from reading. I could only see the broken characters, the bad backing-up, the patchy gradations of black on the page, the erratic spacings. Decided I'd better leave it to others to make the mistakes: Graham, Alastair, Andrew, Clifford, Will, Ian, Stan, David, Jack, the elected fools, supreme, heroic failures in pursuit of the hairy unknowable. For their sakes I wish I could name it. But they wouldn't want that either. Nothing has stopped.

DOSSIER 1

Jeremy Reed

Some poets disappear like missing planes, more specifically Malaysia Airlines Flight MH370, which disappeared en route from Kuala Lumpur to Beijing on 8 March 2014, believed to have dipped down in seas far west of the Australian city, Perth.

Mr A.B., like the enigmatically elusive Mr W.H., Shakespeare's same-sex attraction in his fridge-shaped sonnets, has temporarily gone under the radar as disinformation. As someone who didn't push and was never pushed, a poet who worked language like decoding a plate of noodles into a 25-line diagram (minus saturated fat) his work still signals to the few including me who recognise his outstanding originality. As a printer typographically setting and spatializing words on the page – Tom Raworth, Jim Dine, David Meltzer, Jack Hirschman, B.S. Johnson etc, Asa's inside track on language gave him a constructivist view of what worked and didn't in the infrastructural design of a poem.

Disinformation: effectively lowering the signal-to-noise ratio of unclosed information channels – black propaganda, countermisinformation team, Operation INFEKTION, these are all tangential integrants to Asa's approach of arresting narrative and dispersing it into fractured splinters. Asa's poems are like infra-bits of architecture that coalesce into poetry so modern as to always exist in the future. It's like each poem is a library of possibilities and for Asa like opening the *I Ching* on momentarily randomised trigrams.

AB the first two letters of Asa's immersion in alphabet soup and the permutations of language coded into his cells. If you'd analysed Asa's DNA it would have been quantified by helical letters. He was locked into language like a pressurised cabin and much of his apparent disillusionment with life came from the fact he couldn't break the loop and get out of the puzzle.

The break with language, however transient, was for Asa the world of visual imagery – he'd buy top shelf magazines from Kentish Town shops – *Playboy, Penthouse, Mayfair* and sort of auto-collage erotic angles into the dense textural mood-board of his poetry. The explicity and luxuriously designed *A Word In Your Season* (1967), an edition of six prints printed silkscreen and letterpress in eight colours on silver boards with haiku by Asa and Jack Hirschman is one example of the erogenously-zoned body mapped into a language that substitutes for sex, so too the illustrated broadsheet 'Change' published by Caligula Books.

Keeping a dead poet alive is a unilateral contract: there's no asking reciprocation on his or her part, and with Asa you always got the impression he really didn't believe that anyone outside a tiny coterie of twenty or thirty people ever read poetry angular to mainstream packaging.

Asa saw bad poetry as like botulism, using his book *Dense Lens* (1975) to initialise association with a bacterium often associated with sausage meat as a point of counterattack, issuing it as a Trigram Botulus Book, with my *Isthmus of Samuel Greenberg* also published under that defiant imprint. It was Asa's asymmetric swipe at the fuckedness quotient of a reactionary British mainstream attempting to block Black Mountain influence and the liberated Ashbery New Yorkers putting a campari colour into modernism. Dense Lens like Edge published in the same year are the two books seminal to Asa's development of a recognisable style as something totally his own. You can feel Pound's Chinese reinventions coming up in both books as part of Asa's essentially nomadic culture – London was a transitioning base and not a home – and his work situated in imaginary geographies compounding real and altered sites is liberated into something elevatingly individual and quantumised, urban exile and escape into a place built out of language i.e. the poem. That Asa can't shift acute awareness of language as the tool constructing his reality – there's no other basis – means he struggles with writing as an illusion from which he can't get free. Everything comes back to this criterion and the confusion of the arguable multiple permutations you can give a poem, and why is one mix better than another? Once you start thinking that it's a pathway to madness. Asa spent a lot of time on the poem's compass debating traffic moves, and if *AtoZ* was one way in it was arguably too hermetic demanding he break out.

Whiskey didn't help the process either; it reminded him of so many casualties burnt by the bottle. Hart Crane, Scott Fitzgerald, Malcolm Lowry, B.S. Johnson whacking it solitary in Islington: Asa's glass placed on a marble surfaced table – a printer's edge – was often a drop into cataloguing parasuicides and suicides through an amber meniscus. Weldon Kees, who disappeared off Golden Gate Bridge in 1955 and for whom Asa wrote 'Umbrella', was another missing poet dropped into the sea without trace.

What did Asa and Bryan Johnson, two disaffected north Londoners talk about when they went fishing on the Hampstead ponds, brooding on life, loss, marital discord and language in dark ponds? Asa's design for B.S. Johnson's *Poems Two* is significantly black as the mood integrated into the poetry, as the distillation of Bryan's suicide preliminaries with the emphasis on rotting and had it up to there resignation to bad getting worse in domestic and literary affairs. Once you're in that state you start to associate gunge on bathroom tiles with plaque in your arteries. Bryan carved into the network of arteries highwaying his wrists, in a hot bath, having drunk half a bottle of brandy, leaving the other half for whoever found him (Barry Cole) with a message attached 'Barry finish this.' On a card dated 13 November he wrote his last five words 'This is my last word.' More than any of his experimental deconstructed novels *Poems Two* is the stripped-down quintessential Johnson book, the substrate to all the emotional angularity with which he came at life, seventy per cent loss thirty per cent gain. What B.S. Johnson brings to poetry, as a repressed romantic, is a gritty existential realism documenting disillusionment. Less texturally layered than Benveniste, and less linguistically dense, Johnson as a poet is as much about attitude, and a chippy angular one at that, as he is about inhibited lyricism. Both poets appear to mistrust the inherent romanticism in themselves and to put emotional aerobrakes on that impulse, despite the fact both were experiencing marriages that were painfully disintegrating, Asa's with Pip and Bryan's with Virginia. Narrowing in on his self-terminated end Johnson on 4 November 1973 wrote to his Hungarian friend György Novak: 'Now the sad news. My wife left me last weekend; she's back in the house again, but the marriage is no longer a marriage. I am totally shattered, and am trying to pick up the pieces. What happens now? The corrosive inner stress of Johnson's writing deadlines, as a novelist and sports journalist, something from which his poetry remained exempt like an offworld activity – the impulse to write it like a lightwell existing in his damaged nerves – anticipates in its scrunched tone the breakup partly caused by his saturated drinking and partly by a misogyny characterised by stereotyping women. Maybe the poetry he wrote so sparingly was the most intimate Johnson got with himself. It certainly slowed down his hyperactive thought processes unlike fiction that speeded them up. Irascibly pissed off by most things in his daily effort to maintain his life from books that didn't commercially cut it, poetry was a sort of time out for the beleaguered Bryan. 'The Thames at Mortlake' perfectly synthesises the respite he felt crunching over roughed up Thames shingle at low tide, alone to document his own distressed autonomous brain chatter. A big solitary man walking by a green Thames ruffle picking over randomly found objects: the disjecta the river deposits with its own slippery tang as signature.

> the objects to be
> seen
> found

principally (I have it still)
a short fat halfpound brass bolt and nut
virgin, unscrewed

other things less permanent

sodden grey bones
scratched glass, rubbed brick, rusted gatebutts
once a chaffinch eggshell

every conceivable other

but mainly dirty shingle
silt
prairies of malachite slime

though was the important thing
that I met no one else there?

Johnson's forcibly take-it-or-leave-it approach to poetry shared aspects
in common with Benveniste, in that both poets were essentially writing
without a preconceived reader and into the virulent backdraft of mainstream
writing with diffident disrespect for authority, like a Boeing taking off into
another's scorching exhaust.

There's a urinous lemony tang to Johnson's corrosives, as though he
pissed on poetry as the substrate to writing it, or is that how I wish to
conceive of his practice? Johnson's affront, his squared-up misanthropic
misogyny is there in the book's opening poem 'Bad News For Her Mother'
that directs abrasive energies at his wife Virginia, as target.

'Yes, I shall write it all down, you old cow,
all: the first time, the last time, all the times
in between, and than all the times I should
have liked there to have been. I shall go on
writing it all down even out of habit,
till there is nothing left to exorcise.

You may judge from that the emotional
Debt I feel your lovely daughter owes me.'

Stripped of metaphor, a defiant irritant, Johnson's nasty is a controlled venomous squirt, rather than an acid attack, a toxin injected into the nerves as slow-burn poison. *Poems Two*, divided into five sections, Exorcising, Loving, Observing, Unthinking and Rotting provides the potentialities for often disinclined lyric. If Johnson never appeared relaxed in any form – he was aggressive to his subject matter in both fiction and poetry, then his poetry is collapsed into a softer core lyrically than his experimentally inflected prose. It's often the intervention of nature, as it was for Benveniste that inspires lyricism in Johnson, as though his thoughts are more easily invested in the organic rather than in human emotions. Asa too draws on the Norfolk landscape as a physical platform to his imaginary geographies, referencing landscape as the basis to earth his time-slip collage-jumps across variant timelines and cultures.

House Mother Normal: A Geriatric Comedy (1971) of which Trigram Press published a limited edition preceding the trade one from Collins, *Poems Two* and *Christy Malry's Own Double-Entry* (1973) were the last books Johnson published in his lifetime, attempting to offset his inveterate feelings of despondency and alienation by purchasing on hire-purchase an expensive Citroën GS 1220. On Monday 12 November, the car broke down when he was driving through Islington, causing him to pull into a cul-de-sac off Upper Street and abandon the car, almost as a mechanical pointer to the irremediable state of disrepair in which he found himself – vengeful, jinxed, drunk and on the way out. He abandoned the Citroën, which was only discovered weeks later, to walk home and make a last suicidal call to István Bart in Budapest, who recalls: 'Bryan called on the night of his suicide. He was sort of telling me he was going to commit suicide. It was a desperate telephone call, I didn't know what to say, I couldn't say anything, so I sat down to write a letter, because the communication at that time was…Well, after that the telephone didn't answer, there was no other way but writing a letter.'

There wasn't any reversal now and Johnson ran a hot bath, pulling on a brandy bottle, and flooded the water red slicing his wrists. The synthesis of what got this resistant, resilient prolific writer, into that no-exit bath is best discovered in the contents of *Poems Two* as a sort of emotional manual to his truculent sadness and inexhaustible verbal facility. *Poems Two* is Johnson's black book and its five component sections the complex pathways by which he lived, loved, hated, rotted and ultimately got out of it young.

Trigram catalogue descriptions of the limited first editions of *House Mother Normal: A Geriatric Comedy* and *Poems Two*.

B. S. Johnson *House Mother Normal*

In his fifth novel *House Mother Normal* BS Johnson maps out the interior worlds of eight old people and their House Mother as they live through a Social Evening – with bizarre climax. The thoughts and speech of each of the protagonists are given in separate sections, with their own page numbers, so that each event can be followed through eight different minds. House Mother's final version adds yet another remarkable dimension to what has gone before. *House Mother Normal* marks an important development in our concept of the novel form and confirms Johnson's mastery in poetic understanding of the human condition.

Quarter bound in cream and buff Buckrams. Yellow endpapers and silk headbands. Abbey Mills Antique Laid text pages. Clear acetate dust-wrapper.

B.S. Johnson *Poems Two*

Johnson in *Poems Two* is much more at ease than in his 1964 volume. The problems of form have been solved or overcome, and the poems gain in wit and seriousness as he moves closer to the experience which has conjured the poems; indeed closer to the poems which have conjured and informed that same experience. Here is a man concerned with the experience of poetry as it touches every aspect of his living, a man engaged in Exorcising, Loving, Observing, Unthinking and Rotting. These are the five defining sections of his book.

Half bound in two shades of green Buckram. Green Antique Laid endpapers. Abbey Mills Antique Laid text pages. Clear acetate dustwrapper.

EDGE

Asa Benveniste

Asa Benveniste *Edge*

Joe Di Maggio No. 12, 1975, published by John Robinson
from 23 Fairmead Road, London N19.

Edge, the entire text of which is reproduced here, was published by John Robinson using a Gestetner mimeograph machine on white mimeo paper, priced at £2.00 per box of 500 sheets, the text typed onto stencils and stapled using a Rexel Long Arm stapler. Asa brought over the typed manuscript to John's flat, typically dubious that there would be any demand for the book, drank Cutty Sark with him, listened to records by Kenny Wheeler and Norma Whinstone, his favourite female jazz vocalist, as well as to music by Carla and Paul Bley from John's extensively eclectic record collection. Asa personally supplied the wraparound white typographic covers featuring a deliberately blurred slow exposure shot of him taken by Pip Benveniste on a Nikon F. 300 copies of the book were run off, of which 50 were given to Asa, with John filtering copies to recognisable small-press outlets like Compendium, Bernard Stone and Bertram Rota. John remembers Asa filling the room with blue cigarette smoke on his visits and talking of his determination to publish Louis Zukofsky's *A 22 &23* as the terminal book to Zukofsky's epic poem *A*.

Living Unit

You find me counting the number of times
our bodies have crossed in this room
scene change
                    the ringmaster shies
from flying geese the African plain
blossoms into fire
                        and air and beginneth
the word the transcending

The History of Trench Warfare

transcending soft enough a care for contours
travel is not one of the considerations
there are dangers
                              in using old paper
for certain types of poem
somewhere else we are having lunch together
in a focussing distance
                              the Aegean is obvious
by the way we speak

mist lies on the road northward
two feet above the warring plovers
I have caught my ear in her mirror music
the battery runs down the wet banks
of her body
                    being a plain woman
she carries flowers back to earth
and waits for her own language
one of the rules is to keep the head
below water
                    many deaths

Bird Appeal

We are one with nature O!
don't go away rizla never
leave me
            for a start the golden
gouge comes wrapped in ampoules
of mild pain killer for mild
pain
        not as precise as some
social poems perhaps
            or miscellaneous objects

In another description
The sea rages against specific
bananas
            a form of lockjaw
keeps the peanut boats from ever
coming into harbour
                        'craw craw'
the gentle gulls remark
'when will it end?'
say 'when
            NEVER!'
says the intuitive arrow
MAYBE NEVER

To Nudge Avail

off the mirror o dense word hollows
there is much land stubble to get past
before arable which will make sense
of all journeys all seed dwelling
                        what's missing here
is clearly induced narration
the marauding hill tribes
                                rape loot
new taxes and such like
following the suppression of old forms
of dervish
                in favour of language traffic
the lushness of black the appointment
to assist in minor prophecies
how the earth doth profane itself
with architecture
                        and many forms
of close communion
men do not participate in final payment
'I am not concerned with laf after death'
life alters life and in this manner
the earth has eaten upon itself
looking outward to the spin
of nudge availability
                        o tilt
such as now wherever soft
and takes us with ease & readiness
I dedicate to tumbles
                        landfall wind
the deathly sugars incomprehensible humour
snapped branches and all that is done
in divine error

Working with Coypu

mouthful trouble one way to start
finding the only word is adrenalin
in prestigious porcelain the colours
are arranged the following way
yellow cyan magenta black
and white as a repetitious printing
when suddenly the sun shines
one millimetre ahead of the speeding
eye twinkle dead honey many targets

this explains the pica rule
conquistador hero returning home
with shoes of thin beaten gold
from dust farmer to god
the dark deepens the windowless temple
outside buffalo stampedes have reduced
the exploding coypu to a survivor
referable word hiding in the gutter
another baby added to the rain figures

Boil

American Midwest my plentiful pain
God he cries out if you let me off
with this last one in the armpit
growing like slag I promise to follow
with definitely improved camera work
so much oil underfoot the land
is boiling over with damp richness
buffalo shoes anarak chairs and girls
who haven't heard of sex altogether
but plan ahead anyway as though
the quality of autumn rust coloured
fixing fences as close as they can get to Ohio

At night I take the other lines up with me
and place them strategically correct
in pairs of local confusion as birds
who find their dead places on the road
late spring young out of warm ruffles
flying along my eyes blink much these days
collision turning point subject matter
edges are as sharp as you find them

The Finger Points to Humid

cloud certainty with occasional square
the repetitious dream the repetitious shape
I begin that awesome heroism   divination

the flood of earthy nomenclature
revising all the river ocean lake references
whenever birds come in under the door
dying with legends totally on the page
                              such as Shenandoah
weather condition (such as) sharks infest
turning point
                  the water turns

that side of holy Wensum where is a use
of papier-mâché rock with palm trees
crinkling away to humid and followers same
                              it's the age
we live in says the river like nothing else
swelling to overtake combustion engines
engaged over surfaces of car park
                              the endurance
of aqueous a stormy tranquillity of skies
opening up the knife edge of change

Sonatina

The leg drops down – munch!
                    strikes the first
what am I looking for?
enthusiasm is one thing you can say
about court music
in this area the east wind
when it isn't threatened by stubble fire
zips in on time
                    you notice monosyllables

pars secunda
inaccuracies of language
I put this down to an event
in my image susceptibilities
and now to conclude
we have uncovered
                    this time
so munch
and
no
more

It's the Same Old Feeling Again

The Jealousies
We start by knowing what glues together
and what locks without the aid of circuits
it's important to fly throughout the body
of information iron railings on my left
other runners already spots against
my right arm kissing each word
as it emerges from the image spark
this is something to do with collision
in the face of extreme pleasure
and a way to get round the new seasons
whichever decencies happen to follow

The Decencies
Lie together is already an ambiguity
easier to face easier to avoid
she understood everything he said
they looked to the front door to break
a noisy exchange of reference
plastic models airplane vintage poem
old windy waiting stage the point is
sunlight streams through to the design
and effects the music traversing its way
into the life of my audial bushes
yes

Railway Poem

enter & ride this particular poem for example
inevitably turning left round the railway junction
the most beautiful girls are those
who gyrate in free boredom
episodically with welcome arms
and open sandwich courses

                          Mother

as you can see I have discarded
those origins except as a simple echo
of my father's voice my father's voice
spring is beginning to appear
in my armpits as an adequate terminus
within the contest of seasons
late mourning the absent gesture towards

                                Prince Chou

at this moment running the coins
somewhere under the eyes of his almond wife

Certainly Metaphysics

In certain descriptions I notice certain words occur
over and over unassailed non-argumentative benign
I am not afraid to play the part of Chinese emperor
and do not believe it is the easiest way to wisdom
there are some shapes we fill without entering into
for example language is one of the body limitations
for example my engagements outnumber my pleasures

That said I have to begun to realise already
this is one of the key poems one of the description poems
outside this room in which we get extremely good reception
it will almost certainly snow although I hesitate
what appear to be certain floating fragments
in the air similar to the outline anatomies
similar to certain religious encroachments

Specifically Sexual

So finally we approach the last haunches
wavy lines that go out to the pilotte
amorous is the most meaningless
of all
        Oh God everybody tells me
to keep it simple
                        still
my mouth is beginning to have a life of its own

with several more English to follow
in stupefaction I watch the worm
go down on her hairy epithet
always shifting incorrigible metaphors
just one simple image and then
                                        well…
the impression stick falls continuously
at the wrong time
                        she comes to me now
through the field of Chuang Tzu's
second stanza
                the illusionary fishes poem

Poem

1 THE TEXT

He does not want this to have any connection
with Chinese poem all about calligraphy
rain on his cube of ink he writes
'cloud slants across the Greater Rockies
reflection of good life on earth scars the face'
somewhere along the sequence of earlier heaven
a poem has to have

2 THE COMMENTARY

'rain on the cube of ink'
he speaks of his diminishing powers
and how often his (and others) death
one way the light changes tracing
the carnal comforts from east to south
to north
        reflection nice word
for loyal servant
NEVERTHELESS
a poem has to have a certain solemnity

A Manual for Pilots

As it goes without saying
wind at the side of house
garbage or be careful to weigh
the serious implications of dreams
Signal for first flood of colour

The blah blah click splash penetration
five p.m. rain and then it's caution
for undue influence of numerology
lovelife allied subjects

At this point the Duke of Chou
to remind us that less rhetoric
a true effort towards more image
the long roman wall around Essex
ice as they say beginning to 'form'
on the southerly trigrams

What can he do with all that dust?
there are so many American poets
(I mean pilots) just waiting
on the back of tomorrow's tortoise
in jasmine corridors who question
after question

Meet Mish Mush

or Hokusai those blue sunshine strokes
they say who speaks to waiting doors
starting the dream off with rhythm
blue rain blue smoke blue eyes
I've seen her fill the grand canal with birds
before the great release a slag
of poems obscures the view inside
'I honour Mish Mush in any medium'
he says mourning his resinous lunch
'she's mind mind all mind'

for Tom

The Greek Anthology

Don't bother me with Heraclitus
that reveals a fragmentary greatness
of thought
            moving on to Li Po
who tipped his ass at the moon
and fell into a bucket shop in Baltimore

I cannot justify anything
concerning Demeter goddess of corn
as long as connections are being made
and since we're out in the country
falling under the Virgilian sky
in the distance those lights
are a tall end of the province
of Delaware
            being crossed
by the crazy dactyl Washington
but I don't really see it myself

Middletown, Virginia

The geography of roses?
I remember Bezalel Loew
accumulated so much rubbish
in the cellar and up they came
leaving their mark on this inn
of distinction enough to last
all those generations ago
there have been many transmutations
since the breakthrough in Bombay duck
dimpled paper yes footprints on
the clock tower yes a nasty time
and today there is so much length
of white dog loping loose in the ice
cream parlour when silver propelling
pencils have just disappeared
out of our lives the older I get
the more etcetera
                  there's no end at all
to the number

Cours de Civilisation Française

I cannot help it
if one line follows
on logically
from the next
regard the purity
of tone the placement
of each phrase inevitably
upon the forthcoming
mouse mickey french
the secret life
of Paul Fort
not forgetting
bears throughout Paris
who recently enthused
over crime passionnel
and from the first mouthful
they spoke
    poulet surprise

First Words

I don't remember writing the word Christendom before
and except for 'tribe' won't trouble you
with OED definitions

                          other words come to mind: however
is one of them: cocktail: temperature falling:
cunnilingus: power failure –

                              but 'armoire'
is closer to the truth: ah! the efficacy
of transformation: the ability to transcend
ethnic differences: la lune for example belongs to
Houston Texas and the tricks some poets play
on their wives

                   I love you Maud
I hope we meet sometime quickly
on the way to Wimbledon

New Writing

With the best intention I am about to start
a description of lions who sun themselves
in the black gorse at nightfall gather gather
draws his arm across sweat there's hardly time
before the next poem the river the girl in that order
who cannot wait to give herself completely to ice
the distance between pâtisseries that's real travel
awake during the inverted commas of open space
the sea washes up hanging so much dust along the hammering
eye the haunches the burning thicket the ancient mound
of her belly the two constellations the milky way
of her throat the tongue of song in her mouth
                                        I tell you
I never want to escape the book of words
no matter how much love is showered upon my mane

Key

One familiar two familiar etcetera
I've used them often every day
hardly any colour releases the middle door
at home and once in an emergency
opened the petrol tank though I tried
that before I came and failed

                                    a bad way
to start

Setting the Scene
Sat with you before you left
into the corners of my eyes
quiet potman (old english) soft
arab slippers picked one key
(bags of instinct) out of twenty
on the ring opening a cupboard
of irish whisky

                    no hesitation at all
& that's what really happened
in my dream

Part Five
Walked up steps to front door

                        opened outward
unexpected lights on all over the house
flashing music from central chimney
dashed down one corridor

                        rooms either side
and out the back

                sunlight

                      grass lying flat
and another
room
walked up   front door
each house opened into sunlight
grass lying flat on the ground

Biography of the Poet

Everyone thinks in keys
sunlight referred to many times
not once devourer of plants& water
I want to say colour eating colour
cannibal snail iridescent at my door
with a first collection of calcific poems
too late for poet of the sixties
but he might make magician his crown

Later
Small traces of number & letter
                         gematria
'shot through with figures
from the chivalric tradition
this fine simile
midrash to Ruth referring
to the Torah as a nut'
                    ten minutes
to get through the 45 concealments of God
the house (again) applauds like a crazed
                         orchard of birds
                         planted in broken glass

Further Reading
of sunlight's
for example

The Wild, The Awful, The True

Suddenly that greed of poetry
a damp smell from the bricks
                    (brickwork)
as I emerge from sleep
right up to signs of rain
or failing that to signs
of cattle

The race is about to multiply
Schopenhauer at the roadside
counts little cars that use the A145
with mother sunshine in the tree
that died about a hundred years ago
That's philosophy That's Life
I'm beginning now to tell
you about the awful dream
Looked up diagram of girl & other sections
the noise of chairs
                    do you remember?
like ships unload cackling dog?
all those limitations?
I refrained from writing poems
yesterday the light sent the wind
                         (downtrack)
Break (close) turn away
she rises from the sacrifice in fragments
length of line determined by paper
dimensions of page
                         heart disease
I work myself into a priest
even the grass
              is a dotted line

Who Left The Door Open

Yellow paper conceals akkadian scribe
(o English landscape
once in every poem)
again
(o englische landschaft
une fois chaque poeme)
navigation by blind goddess
he ruins his sleep
testing purities of water
cylinder seal 2.5 centimetres
high again at side of page
and assumes a seasonal mask

still with too much syntax
Finished for today he takes cap in hand
screws it over writing edge
reads telegram thus:
YOU HAVE BEEN CO-OPTED
TO GENERAL COUNCIL
LINE SPACE
or thus:
CONGRATULATIONS FATHER OF
ELEVEN POUND BABY ASTEROID
LINE SPACE
and notes connection
between this and subjective
weight at birth
o signature of sender

Title Poem from the Author's Posthumous Collection, *Healthy Cake*

He tenders his gland together
with 0.5 pollen of daffodil – no, 0.8
ah! science! I address you with the fact
that lethal gas rises from the five books
of splendour in the morning
post everywhere announcing
the herons have begun to leave
the province of Choan
You come early and I wish to say
you are a part of
the conflict in my mind
the neighbours voices as well as that
get nearer and pause before
the visitors recite Aragon
they chip away at the house
with cake knives
                              beautiful day
to land on the moon
I hear them advance
the sheer skill of sequence
chip chip I'm back again
to reveal desultory things
about Spain
                    Aragon! salaud

DOSSIER TWO

Jeremy Reed

1965 × 3

When Asa Benveniste set up Trigram Press in 1965, at an optimal time in London's emergent pop-identified youth culture, he was part of a spearheading triumvirate of independent publishers, who attempted to radically liberate British poetry from its iffy, flat down-sized mediocrity by the booster energies of a distinctly American branded poetry freed-up by its angle on the rapidly-transitioning modern world. Contemporaneous with Asa's starting point, Barry Hall and Tom Raworth were busy collaborating on Cape Goliard in a disused cobbled stable behind Finchley Road tube station, and the Rhodesian born Stuart Montgomery had an eye out for the Black Mountain influenced poets Robert Duncan, Gary Snyder and Ed Dorn, as the shaping influence on his pioneering innovative Fulcrum Press. Montgomery alone of the three wasn't a printer, instead contracting the work out to Villiers Press, but integral to the cover art sourced from the likes of Tom Phillips, Barnett Newman, Patrick Caulfield, Ron Kitaj or Richard Hamilton, all helping distinguish Fulcrum books from mainstream trade editions. The emphasis on a new look for poetry through visually compelling cover art, in the way that Mods had created the look in street fashion, distinguished all three resistantly cutting edge presses. Trigram were arguably on the frontline due to Asa Benveniste's exceptionally virtuoso flair as an unconventional typographer, with a fashionista's shock sense for colour-coded endpapers, and an unparalleled design feel to give Trigram books the same sort of visual appeal as record sleeves as an undisputed first for poetry. As a working partnership Asa Benveniste and his stepson Paul Vaughan combined to create the singularly most original letterpress printed books ever fed into the chain, with their habitual 26 signed and lettered limited editions pushing the collector's genre beyond the limits of preconceived expectation. Asa's generosity to his authors in supplying liberal free copies of their book on request was both part of his natural kindness and also in part motivated by his self-effacing belief that poetry was largely commercially unsaleable and only read by the people who'd already been given the book to help get it some sort of conducive readership. Asa was convinced this didn't spread very far, and I remember when he turned down John Ashbery's *Three Poems*, a decision he later regretted, him telling me that the English were totally closed to this sort of postmodern textural window. Asa didn't like a lot but he agonised over rejections.

And why Trigram, as a sort of cryptic mathematics, a pointer to *Ba gua*, a philosophic concept in ancient China, a trigram is also linguistically a group of consecutive written units such as letters, syllables or words, as well as conceptually eight figures formed of three parallel lines, each either whole or broken, combined to form the sixty-four hexagrams of the *I Ching*. Asa inherited in different permutations all of THAT?

London in 1965 was a capital accelerating into global focus as the turbulent dealing room for brokering cultural change. The pop charts as the enviable acme of youthful rebellion were dominated in part by the ubiquitously popular Beatles and the sneeringly intransigent Rolling Stones as two differentiated aspects of pop, domestic and rogue. As outlets for Trigram, Cape Goliard and Fulcrum there was initially the flagship Better Books, founded by the British publisher Tony Godwine at 94 Charing Cross Road in 1964, and Bernard Stone's Turret Bookshop at 1 Kensington Church Walk, a tight book-lined, book-stashed oblong squeeze in which unmeasured vodka and orange was the brain-numbing house drink. In September 1965 John Dunbar, Peter Asher and Barry Miles opened Indica Books and Gallery in Mason's Yard, off Duke Street, St James', as another counterculture hub, closely associated with the Beatles that would benefit the formative new poetry independents in their attempt to reach a younger pop-influenced demographic. To consolidate the quotient of three adventurous outlets for three avant-garde publishers, Compendium Books at 240 Camden High Street, founded by Nicholas Rochford and Diana Gravill was to open in August 1968, as perhaps the single most influential core for a youth dynamic busily integrating music and drugs into the detail of literature. 1965, the year in which Asa Benveniste published Oswell Blakeston's *How To Make Your Own Confetti*, on confetti coloured paper with drawings by Max Chapman, was succeeded by the publication the following year of Asa's own first book of poetry *Poems of the Mouth*, with drawings by Pip Benveniste. Of the poems inherently obscure relationship with language as a sort of process of divination, Asa wrote: "The Chinese considered the mouth the paramount aperture of the body. God breathed life into Adam. The Hebrew Kabbalists believed the utterance of certain sounds so important that some were completely prohibited. The earliest experience of love is oral. Sustenance is taken in the mouth. Speech is the most common form of communication, and we all die first in the mouth... It was only after writing these poems over the past two years that I realised they were linked by the word of mouth."

By publishing Oswell Blakeston, essentially a quirky gay detective-fiction writer, and a maverick poet, Benveniste was initializing what would be a prevailing interest on his part in minimal, jokey surreal compression. Blakeston's short splinter poems being the lead into an experimental genre mined by the likes of Tom Raworth and Anselm Hollo as future Trigram poets and pushed out to cooler edges of sixties playful dare.

If Trigram's 1965 books failed to dent public awareness, then Fulcrum Press won surprise attention by the critical acclaim surrounding the publication of Basil Bunting's *Briggflatts*, a rehabilitated Northern poet, who Asa regarded as too formulaically English to sit with his Americanised tastes – too stuck in nostalgic evocation of landscape to excite his sensibilities. But as a slice of collaborative publishing history, the first printing of *Briggflatts*, designed by Stuart Montgomery, was printed by Barry Hall and Tom Raworth at the Goliard Press on Trigram's larger Glockner flat-bed cylinder press, hardback bound in black buckram, green laid paper dustwrapper printed in 72 Caslon and limited to 500 copies, of which 26 were specially bound, lettered and signed by the author. Instrumental in putting Fulcrum on the poetry map, *Briggflatts* was a decidedly non-Trigram affair with Asa's personal interests more idiosyncratically rooted in Louis Zukofsky's demandingly complex language-poetry expressed through his universally scoping epic, *A*.

In 1966 when Benveniste published George Andrews' psychedelic poems, *Burning Joy*, the imagery saturated by marijuana and LSD molecules, the book was actually jobbed out to Hall and Raworth, with Barry Hall providing a cover painting; the book set in 12" Monotype Centaur, 550 numbered copies, with 50 hardbound and signed by the author. Burning Joy signposted Trigram's mid-sixties arrival in a London transitioning musically and metabolically from rhythm and blues to psychedelia, speed to LSD as pharmaceutical morph, with Jimi Hendrix's virtuoso wah-wah facility instigating changes not only in music, but also poetry, despite concerted mainstream opposition to psychedelics as hallucinated pathways to vision. Already a smoke academy from American brand cigarettes Asa's own recreational drugs tended to be smokeable psychoactives: hashish, cannabis, marijuana. Interestingly, in 1967 George Andrews and Simon Vinkenoog were to edit *The Book of Grass*, an anthology of drug writings that included Burroughs, Trocchi, Ginsberg, Bowles, Henry Miller etc, as the definitive anthology of its kind.

Any notion of Trigram ever going normal was quickly dispelled by the publication of Piero Heliczer's *Soap Opera* in 1967, the poems illustrated by Andy Warhol, Wallace Berman, Jack Smith, Jean-Jacques Lebel and Paul Vaughan etc , the book bound in purple cloth stamped with silver, with an illustrated orange dust-jacket, printed letterpress by Benveniste in an edition of 500 copies, the first sixty numbered and signed.

Piero Heliczer, an experimental film-maker and part of Warhol's Factory amalgam had made art-house movies like *Satisfaction, Venus In Furs, Joan of Arc* (in which Warhol appeared), as well as an unfinished three-hour epic, *Dirt*, and published his own books through The Dead Language Press he'd founded specifically for this purpose. Heliczer came to Benveniste's attention through Tom Raworth, whose Matrix Press had jointly published Heliczer's *And I Dreamt I Shot Arrows In My Amazon Lover's Bra* with The Dead Language Press in 1963, with Raworth zoning in on Heliczer's endemic use of lower case even for titles, and his often discontinuous film-like narrative to theme his ambiguously sexed hyperreal poems. *Soap Opera* is pop poetry, and Heliczer was the only contemporary poet to write about Stephen Ward's suicide, a death precipitated by the Profumo affair, erotically empathising with Ward's confused sexual relations with Christine Keeler: "I made beautiful love to you leaving purple/ and green bites on the inside of your thighs." Heliczer's personally chaotic life – he died in 1993 – meant that much of his unplaced creative work was irremediably lost. He was associated with the Velvet Underground through Andy Warhol, Gerard Malanga, and the musicians, Tony Conrad and Angus Maclise, with whom he collaborated on the soundtrack for his movie *Autumn Feast*, shot by Jeffrey Keen.

Trigram's development as a press fully and collaterally integrated into the radically transitional morphs happening in sixties visual art, was confirmed in 1968, when Benveniste published Anselm Hollo's *The Coherences* with drawings by Tom Phillips, and Tom Raworth's *The Big Green Day* with a dust jacket and illustrations by Jim Dine, both books carrying Benveniste's individuated artisanal signature as a maverick printer/designer who would atypically print the word *Green* on Raworth's *Big Green Day* dust jacket in lipstick red. *The Big Green Day* was Raworth's second book, the successor to Goliard's *The Relation Ship*, arguably his most sustained and pioneeringly innovative book, with Raworth's facetious tendency towards the flippant and the ludic already beginning to show up in a way that seriously scattered his talent. 100 copies of *The Big Green Day* were signed by Raworth and Dine in a book notable for a design intended to be visually attractive and distinctively modern, unlike the plain typographic dust jackets favoured by mainstream poetry publishers of the time like Faber & Faber, Macmillan, OUP and Secker and Warburg.

My close friend John Robinson remembers making several visits to Asa at 147 Kings Cross Road, in the late sixties, initially having sent him a fan letter and being subsequently invited over. John remembers a small self-contained cube-shaped building on two-floors with a yard at the back and the street being integrated into an unprepossessing lowlife quarter with the attraction being cheap rent. Dressed in a black leather jacket, black polo neck jumper, dark blue jeans and black Chelsea boots Asa was islanded by uncut sheets of *Work from the Same House*, the book of photographs and etchings by Jim Dine and Lee Friedlander that he was in the process of publishing, offering John copies of *Residu 2*, an anthology Trigram had published, from the piles of unsold stock, and any of the uncut sheets he cared to take. Asa was at the time so physically undermined by the exhaustion of letterpress printing, and the lack of any commercial gain for Trigram Press, that he was seriously considering selling the concern to John Morgan, who worked part-time at Better Books and was so enthusiastic about the Trigram imprint that he attempted unsuccessfully to negotiate a loan to take it over. John remembers Asa sitting as he often did, cross-legged on the floor, smoking, soaking up the ambience of printer's ink and an obdurate flat-bed press, before suggesting they go out to a small Greek restaurant nearby to eat humus, pittas and dolmades – stuffed vine leaves – a favourite with Asa. On several occasions they combined visits to Compendium Books, so warmly personalised by Nick Kimberley, to pick up what was new in American small press poetry, with going to Marine Ices at Chalk Farm, both attracted particularly by the colour and flavour of pistachio ice cream, followed in Asa's case by black Turkish coffee.

Trigram's optimal output peaked in 1969, with the publication of seven books that helped compound the press into London's coolest avant-garde imprint, and particularly distressing to Asa, as he often told friends, was the persistent repeat submissions of manuscripts by individuals including friends, who he'd turned down already, and whose obduracy was like a stalker's obsession with achieving publication. Asa used to despair over this inveterate tedious pushiness, something that helped contribute to his increasing disillusionment with being a publisher who was singularly responsible for reading all work submitted to Trigram, a disquiet that had him appoint John Keys as a part-time editor in the period 1971-73. The one poet Asa seriously wished to publish, the partially schizophrenic drug casualty Harry Fainlight, who had actually delivered a manuscript to him at King's Cross Road, and within hours turned up asking for its return due to acute paranoid reasons dictated by the voices in his head, was a loss he deeply regretted. In his short, disruptively troubled life, Fainlight's only consent to publication was the small collection *Sussicran*, published in an edition of 150 copies in 1965 by Bernard Stone's Turret Books. With the exception of Paul Gogarty's *Snap Box*, an immediate impromptu decision on Asa's part, most Trigram books evolved from Asa's express interest in a particular poet's work leading in time to the making of a book. 1969 saw the publication on Trigram's part of three essentially cabalistic books of poetry – *Yesod* by David Meltzer, *Black Alephs* by Jack Hirschman and Asa's own *AtoZ Formula*. In addition there was *Welcome Home Lovebirds* by Jim Dine, *At Thurgarton Church* by George Barker, *October* by Nathaniel Tarn and *Work from the Same House* by Jim Dine and Lee Friedlander. The inclusion of two books by Jim Dine, and what was in fact Lee Friedlander's first book upped Trigram's association with counterculture art, while George Barker's, elegiac, self-illustrated rumination on death was a reminder of Asa's lifelong admiration for Barker's pitched visionary firepower that went its own way independent of fashion. Superbly illustrated with drawings by Paul Vaughan, Nathaniel Tarn's *October* is arguably his most lyrically inventive sequence, suffused by an orange autumnal glow which transitions through the book's reflective tempo. 1969, Year of the Cock, placed Trigram on the frontline of the attempted poetry revival that rarely translated into sales, only limited prestige amongst enthused aficionados. But it's Jim Dine's highly experimental first book of poems, *Welcome Home Lovebirds,* that perhaps most flavours the end of the sixties as an epoch of manic cultural acceleration, almost overtaking itself in the process of arriving. In Dine's poem 'In a Green Suit' he signals. "The energy this is taking equals the sensation of making this period." Jim Dine's poems deserve consideration as some of the sixties' best. 'April Weekends' has that just off-focus angle of exposure like a post-drug leftover way of seeing that I personally so admire in work that discovers poetry as its identity rather than making any concessions to preconceived formality.

> 'Tiny gray dots make evening go quick
> You can't ride back to life magazine alone
> Suddenly the gloom which weighs so much is laden
> Full of wet air and is burned so badly by the yellow bowl
> That now flowers (which once bent almost) seem to make
> A winter pouch billow off the pane of daylite'

Inflectively post-modern, abstract, unartily arty, Dine gets that sort of highpoint moment just right, the subject doesn't have to mean, it just feels good, a yellow bowl in flower and an intended daffodil hitting its optimal, so energised it appears literally to bounce off the light it meets. There's bits of Ashbery's casual tone here in making the facility sound easy when it isn't and providing a lyrical curve to a figure that is angularly resistant to arriving. Dine invents his own laws for poetry, in the sense he starts without preconceptions of what is expected and launches in. The results are wonderfully liberating.

'In the country of me there is a lot of dumbness and rage
said the sandpit at the top of the street
i build new houses to clean up the language
where will it go all up the window?'

It's much to Asa's credit that he treated Jim Dine's poems as poetry, and not as an adjunct to his constantly morphing explorations as a visual artist, but as actual writing and Dine's first book of poetry is largely forgotten for that, an excursion into language as linguistic emotion in Ithaca, NY, 1967, and London, 1968, where most of the state-altering poems in *Welcome Home Love Birds* were written. They're as modern and free-form as you'll get for the times, erotic, self-questing, coolly personalised, often visceral and sometimes resembling mini- home videos in their compressed elliptic documentation.

'The prettiest thing about now is that it's all over.
Where do you keep all the things
That don't fit in your mind?
What if they stick out the ends of your hair?'

Poetry was really happening for Dine, not only as part of generational weird, but as the opening out of his response to time and place and where he fitted in both. Letterpress printed by Asa Benveniste and Paul Vaughan and set in 12 on 14 Monotype Joanna, and printed on Broadwell cartridge paper, there was also a signature edition of 100 copies on Basingwerk white parchment, specially bound and containing an original screenprint by Jim Dine. The cover photographs of Jim Dine on the jacket were by Nancy Dine and are of Jim Dine front and reverse image looking into an oval mirror surrounded by the cluttered random paraphernalia of his studio.

The book is in fact the perfect sixties artefact, contents and production to a decade ending as extrovertly innovative as it arrived, like exploding a can of orange Dulux paint into a swimming pool of psychedelics. Writing to Jim Dine at the time of the book's going to the typesetters, Asa was full of his usual apprehensive perfectionism. "Just spoke to the typesetters about your book and they tell me (they always tell me) that proofs should be ready on Thursday. But don't pin too much faith on it. What's holding them up is the display fount for the titles I asked for, although I don't really need those yet. Anyway, soon as we have them I'll stick'em down on pages and pass them on. Yes, I think overlays might be best for the marginalia."

Jim Dine's second book from Trigram, *Work from the Same House* (1969), a collaboration with Lee Freidlander evolving out of the exchange of etchings and photos, came with the accent on the sort of accidental synchronicity that leads to inspired, pointy collaborations, rather than ones in which deliberate contrivance is apparent. According to Jim Dine the two had met in 1962 and begun spontaneously hitting off creative ideas against each other. 'He gave me a photograph of Cincinnati without knowing that I am from there. We have been exchanging things all the time since then. Friendship and pictures. Our work is from the same house.' But Lee Friedlander's reclusive, off-map, difficult personality, provided real problems for Asa, who confided to Jim Dine in a letter: 'Well, I finally heard from Lee Friedlander and I'm frightened. I'm beginning to wonder if the book will ever get past proof stage. A whole list of things we got to do in order to get the maximum accuracy; screen, paper, pigment, varnish, pressure. I mean I don't think we're that good. It's just a hobby with us anyway. I don't want to be a professional printer for god's sake! I love the way you and Lee are trying to get the book into 3000 homes from Modart to Fresno, but I may crack under the strain of getting every single print just as it was christened. What with everything else, like Nixon, Vietnam, China, black power, Stuart Montgomery, the weather and my declining prostate gland.'

Interestingly, Asa didn't print the book and is credited only with typography, the trade edition paperback only, with carnation pink endpapers being printed and bound by W&J Mackay & Co Ltd, Chatham, Kent, the physical specifics noted as "Blocks by MacKay Engraving Co, Text set in 'Monotype' Bell, Titles in Baskerville Old Face and Old Face Open, Paper Ambassador White Art Double Crown 70lbs, design by Asa Benveniste." In addition to the trade edition there was a portfolio edition limited to seventy-five sets published by the Petersburg Press. London. Possibly the most collectable of Trigram books, it was also one of the few to sell out, indicative of Friedlander's erotically themed shots and obsessive fetish with department store windows counterpointed by Dine's bold similarly sexualized etchings, the two tangoing with the sexually liberated times drenched in hormonal uptake.

1970, the opening of a new decade still saturated in sixties psychedelic slapback was a low-tempo year for Trigram, with only one title, Tom Raworth's playfully experimental *Lion Lion* issuing from the press, as a further distancing on Raworth's part from mainstream tracks, through his increasingly elliptical disconnective lyric poems, compressed into allusions the poem deliberately never pursues. While the book's squat rectangular design and layout was unmistakably Benveniste's the book was printed for Trigram by Daedalus Press, Stoke Ferry, Norfolk, in three editions: paperback, cloth and a signature edition of one hundred copies bound in faux python buckram and numbered and signed by the author. Raworth's increased dissociation from a poetry involved in real or described events into one of synaptic speed between imaginative clips is brought into full on collision with the reader in *Lion Lion*, as the template for a work of splintered minimalism best exemplified by *Moving* (1971), a superbly designed, Joe Brainard-illustrated Cape Goliard book, and *Act* (1973), as his Trigram successor. Raworth had arrived at his own signature weird in his textual discussion of rapid detail. Raworth's art is always to tell you what you don't know rather than to confirm what you do – the process of most formalised poetry. 'South America' really gets Raworth's law-breaking transgressive method right on as off-the-wall writing.

> 'he is trying to write a book he wrote years ago in his head
> an empty candlestick on the windowsill each day
> of his life he wakes in paris to the sound of vivaldi in summer
> and finds the space programme fascinating since he still
>   doesn't know
> how radio works as in the progress of art the aim is finally
> to make rules the next generation can break more cleverly '

And one thanks Raworth for breaking the rules so radically, fucking linear progression into how thought patterns as the brain's electric impulses really fire up, transitioning between autonomous visual frames, without the sort of concrete resolution that mainstream poets pretend in making an authoritatively neat conclusion to a poem never intended to end that way.

Raworth's poems mess with systems like opening up disused tube stops on London underground.

In the same year Asa printed Bill Butler's *Byrne's Atlas* for Larry Wallrich, who had relocated from New York's Phoenix Bookshop to a location on Museum Street and – in the line of Bernard Stone's Turret Books – had set up Larry Wallrich Books for the publication of small-press books of poetry. Butler's long episodic poem hacked out of Charles Olson's notions of geography, or psychogeography, was never a Trigram book, although it erroneously enters Trigram checklists and bibliographies. Bill Butler, the founder of Unicorn Bookshop in Brighton in 1967, and with it Unicorn Press, was an openly gay, subversive counterculture antagonist, and responsible for publishing books such as William Burroughs' *Ali's Smile* (1971) and more controversially J.G. Ballard's *Why I Want to Fuck Ronald Reagan*, one of the books for which he was prosecuted under the Obscene Publications Act, when police raided his bookshop on 16 January 1968, taking away over 3,000 items – most of them being copies of *Oz* and representing more than seventy titles. Butler, who lost the case, was left with a bill of over £3,000 that he couldn't meet, but continued to maintain Unicorn Bookshop until it closed in 1973.

1971 again found Asa contracting his elegantly self-designed books out to Juliet Standing's Daedalus Press for the job of printing, as an admission that the physically debilitating process of letterpress on his skinny physique was becoming too much. Never wholly satisfied with the results, his instantly recognisable design skills more than compensated for keeping Trigram's profile optimally charged as arty, pointy books that were always unpredictable as book-candy. Of the books Trigram published in 1971, *The Gavin Ewart Show*, an unexpected concession to conventional poetry flavoured with salacity, was a commercial success, while books by two novelists who were close friends, the limited edition of B.S. Johnson's *House Mother Normal* and, interestingly, Barry Cole's *Vanessa in the City*, were both books by pioneering underlords. Cole's *Vanessa in the City*, a sort of anti-narrative discursive poem full of that sort of enquiry into the meaning of language, rather than direct continuity of theme, is an engaging overlooked work, open field in its exploration and urban in its compass.

Words add only when
the first have been passed, have
to be recollected to fabricate
a comprehensible whole, like my

describing a visit to the hair
dresser or having the heels of my shoes
renewed while I wait, a good
test of patience.

Most poetry simply disappears like Boeing exhaust dispersed into the
atmosphere. There's no coming back on flight path for lost books and
Barry Cole's *Vanessa in the City* is one of those dipped causes, and Asa
felt that about most of his Trigram output that the books were part of
the declassified pandemic called publishing that was in fact anonymous
numbers.

1972 revved up for Trigram, with Asa significantly returning to printing
the books from their new location at 15 Southwark Street, London SE1,
with an eclectic six books published by the imprint that year: B.S. Johnson,
Poems Two, Anselm Hollo, *Alembic*, John Keys, *Hammersmith Poems*, Paul
Gogarty, *Snap Box*, Roberta Berke, *Sphere of Light*, Asa Benveniste/Ray
Di Palma/Tom Raworth, *For the Time Being*. The most interesting of the
new Trigram titles were Paul Gogarty's irreverently pop-ish *Snap Box*, and
John Keys' idiosyncratically psychogeographic *Hammersmith Poems*, as lost
books demanding some sort of retrieval from a poetry mortuary as big as
Harrods in its dead mass of lost causes.

Paul Gogarty's first proper book, a small compact artefact printed blue
on blue was cute, cool and impish, and should arguably have been the
twenty-two year old's debut hit, but it wasn't – instead going underexposed,
under-reviewed, and typically off-radar due to critical contempt for the
book's cryptic, mish-mashed cultural allusions and poems crunched into
minimal compression taking Raworth as their lead. I've an acute fondness
for *Snap Box* both as a design concept, and a kind of cocktail blend of
snappy noted trick poems. The book finds the precocious Gogarty free to
occupy his own weird space of Lewis Carroll meets Confucius under an
English umbrella. The title poem alone sets up the whole bitty elliptical
geometry of poem-bites.

the morning was hard
jane drove her legs again
into the waving candy. she
'd left a piece of toast
in the road

Initialized as his first book of poetry or his last – it was to be his last – *Snap Box* was language poetry at its most allusively playful, like giant buckyballs in molecular collision, and Paul Gogarty or Tommy Oranges, one of its dodgiest exponents. The poetry both should and shouldn't be there, and catches the attention intermittently like accidentally reading a number plate upfront simply as an unaccountable lapse in focus. Gogarty's poems are like foreign number plates slipped into London traffic and interestingly odd. Here's one in the mouth from 'Opus-pocus.'

> Bad Jack Bijou broke dock leaves
> over Baby Zuk the Glow Worm
> grizzling. Tijit, his friend
> and nervous mannequin played Gitu
> the Conch chess. Where these three
> queued, Alderman Justice roamed
> on primed films and rotting pictures.
> It was here that forty Roman box vans
> crowded into Pildegaarde Street;
> here that skill changed Xmenan Forcbessage
> into a turn; here that Nebula Lamper
> made silk cabins from topaz;

This is like *Clockwork Orange* finding an equivalent dialect soup in poetry. Gogarty isn't surreal, he's neon-coloured neologistic, out on his own using a private referential language that literally wings by flippantly as a punchy little insult to the reader who can't attach meaning to the poem. Snap Box causes trouble by its existence as exactly that. It's a book I pull out often to be reminded of the deconstructive morphs poetry can achieve when it breaks all the rules by refusing to acknowledge they even exist. Gogarty's deregulated poetry gives us a sniff of exciting insight into how deeply guarded and inhibitedly restrained the Larkin/Heaney frontline are in their documentation of a pedestrian reality worn out by everyday knowledge of its existence on all our senses. The refusal of the British poetry establishment to endorse experimentation was deeply rooted in an anti-US policy, and the need to block threateningly invasive pathways by the likes of Allen Ginsberg, Frank O'Hara, John Ashbery, Charles Olson, Robert Creeley, Robert Duncan etc in their liberating poetry into uninhibited personal freedom of subject matter – you could write about anything from cocksucking (Wieners) to a raspberry jumper (O'Hara).

Paul Gogarty's *Snap Box* deserves to stand out for rehabilitation to a new generation of British poets still stuck like grainy chewing gum under the foot of a formally unadventurous fifties prototype.

John Keys' *Hammersmith Poems* brought Black Mountain psycho-geography specifically to Hammersmith, as personalised place – the poet's own walkably mapped and internalised pathways of a London base he'd adopted temporarily working as editorial help at Trigram. Using poetry as highgrade information and finding a hybrid trans-Atlantic language Keys meshed into a new investigative poetry, going purposely wide of English malaise, as his idiosyncratic resource. Keys literally fucks place into submission.

> in the bookstore, beneath the sidewalk
> so close to the brown earth
> she walks her footsteps in
> the bookstore beneath the sidewalk
> a cave of words she likes
> very much they have enfolded her
> like soft hummings of bats
> in a belfry so close to
> the brown earth
>
> > O city
> > tumbling over her
> > in purple light

Keys' poetry has that sense of being something ahead that you can't name in American poetry of the early and inside seventies, a sense of fast casual that John Keys picks up on in his London street poems. Keys' alienation rather than exile looks in turn for poet friends who are absent in 'Girls College.' The reassembled can only in turn be presented through imaginative compass.

> maybe it's the way Franz
> Kline would've said
> Right? If he, and my
> poor mangled friend
> O'Hara could have
> come to Hammersmith
> just one little soft

once, and brought Al,
and Walt, and Paul,
and anyone else
who was there

The referencing of influences and friends, Frank O'Hara, Allen Ginsberg, Walt Whitman and Paul Blackburn as an organic resource of getting poetry forward, making it physical through language representing rather than substituting for reality, permeates *Hammersmith Poems* – and has anyone ever written better about Hammersmith as place as launchpad for poetry? And where is the fabulous John Keys – this dossier is an open letter to have him contact poetry again with more books after decades of apparent absenteeism? John, exchange realities; come out of life into language again as circadian rhythm. We need ya, us who work the pathways into wireless imagination where it all happens. Any workable poetics comes out of Pound's whacky disrespect for literature, capital L, and its conversion into disruptive miscegenated origins. Put a Chinese take away translation into a brown paper bag and overwrite it and that's the poem on spaceout: Ez versus dormant Larkin lit + everything written under that redundant moniker. A dose of lysergic acid might have cured the lot.

1973 was a slow-tempo year for Trigram with Asa continuing to print letterpress from 15 Southwark Street, London SE1, and of the two books published that year, Ivor Cutler, *Many Flies Have Feathers*, illustrated by Mary Brogan, and Tom Raworth, *Act*, illustrated by Barry Flanagan, Raworth's work demands attention, both for the book's customised design, and Raworth's continued banditry as a poet outlaw shooting down all logical syntax, or connective associations, between ideas, other than a scrambled coherency shot into largely spatial disorder. When Raworth gets it together to communicate rather than subvert, as in 'Songs Of The Depression', things happen to start for the reader, other than the sense of confused displacement.

there's a shop on the road
we whiz by
slowing down from our speed
a turn off's an angle

talking the song through a kazoo
the giver of which

heads for switzerland
this thought holds it together

It's hard always with Raworth to know if experimentation is cause or effect of the writing, and if unmodified solipsism really ever allows a window for the reader in the poet's speed rush. In 'Gaslight' Raworth's definition of poetry is followed through to some sort of attempted resolution, maybe the closest he's got to describing his art.

poetry is neither swan nor owl
but worker, miner
digging each generation deeper
through the shit of its eaters
to the root – then up to the giant tomato

Contempt for what one does is part of writing – the thanklessness and the wear and tear of importing experiential input into the nervous system as blowout, is all part of the process that reaches a minority, but sticky content readership. If poets stand out it's because the pursuit is so disproportionate to the reward, and the purposed conviction lost on everyone but the few readers who co-partner the journey with inside track knowledge of the inner resources needed to maintain it.

1974 was a block of missing time for Trigram and marked Asa's move to 22 Leverton Street, London NW5, and with it an end to his customised printing of the books, although his exacting, meticulously quirky design skills remained individual to each title. Scheduled for 1975 publication was the Jonathan Williams/Tom Phillips collaboration *Imaginary Postcards,* which due to a disagreement between Jonathan Williams and Asa over the book's layout, resulted in Asa pulling the book from publication, with the 120 copies already bound given away to friends of Trigram Press. The book carried a printed disclaimer reading: 'As a result of a disagreement between the publishers and one of the authors over the design of the book, the publishers have decided not to publish it. Before this decision was reached 120 copies were bound, which are being distributed to friends of Trigram Press.' It was Jonathan Williams' objections that prohibited publication of a book overseen by Asa with design and typography by Donato Cinicolo and printed by Expression Printers Ltd, London N1. Williams' typographical postcards or found poems in the Olsonian sense of place, as interiorised geography, largely originated from a month's hiking the Lake District and the Yorkshire Dales and 'were made with pleasure to give pleasure'; the poet's sensory response to geography implying an emotional attachment to hard physical transitioning. In his Afterword Williams expresses the interior value of landscape and how it benefits the poet's entire circadian organism. 'I haven't seen territory yet that cannot be sexualized; or, examined for its poetic cuisine, or its birds, or for its dialects.'

Williams' found poems and raunchy typographics interact strikingly with Tom Phillips' monochrome images in creating a montaged assemblage. Williams' local reportage is direct and there's little lyrical transformation in his language findings, his diaristic notation of place.

> Looking into One of Three Grikes
> In the limestone pavements of 'Raven Scar'
> Beneath Ingleborough Hill
> We see the Contorted First Three Letters
> Of a Rare Flower's Latin Name,
> And assume the Rest.

The book's perfect dissolve between visual image and gritty text is hard to fault as a product of textual experimentation, and as an image combo ideally suited to Trigram, although Asa's remove from hands-on printing at 22 Leverton Street, the Kentish Town address at which he lived, led to an increasing disengagement from the press. He was also hard put to find books he really wanted to publish, and complained of loneliness, social alienation, the awareness that nobody called him on the phone, and his sense of generally not belonging was additionally intensified by the sharp angles apparent in his marriage. *Imaginary Postcards* was part of the downward spiral of events that was effectively to bring the press to an end in 1978, although the publication of *Dense Lens* in 1975 evidenced Asa's own personal advance, as a largely unrecognised poet, up there with and in many instances ahead of his more recognised underground contemporaries. Printed by Ithaca Press in an edition of 550 paperbound copies of which fifty were signed by the authors and slipcased, the book being stapled with glassine wrappers protecting white printed wraparound card covers, Benveniste's ten poems as part of a collaboration with Brian Marley suggest just how much he had deepened in the personal and domestic content of poems that were no longer just language constructs pointing to cabalistic origins. Asa's typically self-deprecating afterword to his section of the book, 'The Final Focus', downplays the serious merit of his contribution.

'But of all the amazing transmigrations imaginable, the one that pushed this sequence of poems off the ground was something a friend of ours, called Hainsworth, overheard in Audrey's Camden Town pastry shop, when she was seated behind a kind of professional visionary and boot (sic) poet who said to his crumb-filled companion: 'We must get some dream sessions going.' Though before the first poems were ever written the phrase was more or less ancient history. However, I cannot deny that these twenty poems have to remain a homage of sorts to that inspired vapidity.'

The influence of the Confucian aspects of Pound and Zukofsky's precise language-mining are both evident in Asa's new-won confidence in linking the self-reported process of writing to its autonomous opening out into lyric horizons. 'Pound's Planchette' does it perfectly.

> the sequence changing into a seated
> man who converses with a four-inch
> spider scurrying into sunlight stopping
> scurrying stopping
> > the book opens
> folio 232: the apparitions of Miciho Itow

This is *Cantos* diction, the casual transitioning into the classical and the cultural collision left there as an open gateway for the reader to check. For those interested, Michio Itow (1893-1961) was a Nipponese mime and innovative Noh dancer, a friend of Debussy and Rodin in the Paris twenties, and adept through dance at the material significance of the invisible.

The same culturally amalgamated freeing-up equally occurs in the superbly motivated 'Punctuation Enters from the Left', with the apple conceived of as packed with words and presenting the first bite on language as way into naming experience.

> Thus (the motion then being frozen
> it arrived through the door
> just as the apple bite took place
> Alliluyeva or something equally true
> since she is so beautiful
> in the twilight assembly

Disillusioned with publishing and with Trigram critically short of funding, Asa personally compounded a new densely liberated poetry in strict privacy at 22 Leverton Street, work that was rarely externalised unless asked for poems by one of the many small press mimeo magazines in operation at the time. The Trigram Botulus imprint was to be short-lived with only *Dense Lens* and my own Hart Crane-themed *The Isthmus of Samuel Greenberg* (1976), appearing under a moniker implying radical separation from the mainstream. I remember going with Asa one afternoon in 1975 to Bertram Rota on Long Acre and his negotiating the potential sale of signed first editions from his own library, including Paul Bowles, and deciding against it in view of the derisory money offered; but it was indicative of his financial state and the fact the press didn't generate income. But it was for him an improved writing period, both *Dense Lens* and *Edge* published in 1975 are Asa's on the moment books, the central focus of his poetics worked through the language forest into clearer lyrical facility. Like Ashbery, only denser, Asa alludes to bits of his private life that hook the reader, but remain tantalisingly transient, like he's not going to tell you what or where. How to break out of systemised language into reality was what Asa couldn't crack, and he used poetry as the attempt to decode cabala and zone into another dimension of consciousness. That he never found that freedom helped lock him into depression or inflected disappointment, like a Chinaman meditating on a black lotus flower. For Asa the poem's time-slip laminating offers an open window on the page that can't be repeated off.

> the windy Urals also influence
> glucose experiments in Havana and some days
> abandoned to the rain O'Hara gives himself
> to feelings of friendship towards orange and easy
> turns like: the: weeping: mise en scene: thank you

1976 saw the publication of Jeremy Reed, *The Isthmus of Samuel Greenberg*, and Jeff Nutall, *Objects*, as well as the co-publication with Tree Books, Berkeley, of Abraham Ben Samuel Abulafia, *The Path of the Names*, an abstruse kabbalistic treatise that returned Asa to his Jewish origins and the hermetic attributes of language. Obsessed at the time by Hart Crane's marine lyricism, serial debauchery with sailors, Cutty Sark bravado and his suicide by catapulting into the Caribbean from the stern of the Orizaba, my book-length sequence on Crane also named his stated prototype for inspiration, Samuel Greenberg. Greenberg, a New Yorker who died on August 17, 1917, at the age of twenty-three, having endured poverty and deep social isolation, produced a small body of visionary poetry known to Hart Crane in manuscript form, and compared by him to Rimbaud, which was finally published in book form by Henry Holt in 1947 with a preface by Crane's friend, Allen Tate. Drenched in the turquoise, jade and foggy grey light of my island upbringing in Jersey, Channel Islands, I got into the luxury of Crane's visionary sea voyages big time and lyrically stalked him into my poem. It's not anything I'd reprint, as the clustered language inhibits momentum – which you can also argue for Crane – but Asa believed in the poem and chanced on the jacket photo about the time of putting the book into process, the lettering done in violet on a green-grey cloudscaped horizon featuring the Statue of Liberty. I don't think the book got reviewed of even noticed, like most Trigram titles; it just followed the arc of Crane's trajectory into the sea.

Asa's drinking was by now becoming a day-long pursuit, always whisky, J&B, Cutty Sark or simply corner-shop Bells, except when he was with Bernard Stone, and drank Bernard's nuclear bloody marys, a sunset-red spirits bomb that was Bernard's chosen flaming signature. Unable to find work he had any real conviction to publish, another cause of his despair, Asa without much reciprocation took, on Ed Dorn's recommendation, J.H. Prynne's *News of Warring Clans*, as a partial concession to the Cambridge curators of language-poetry that Asa didn't much read, preferring to call it wallpaper. Prynne's enigmatic poem was another dose of Prynne as subjectless avatar of pushing intellectualised paramodern poetry into a highly discerning corner for Cambridge cognoscenti. I, like so many others, read Prynne out of curiosity at the defensive complexity of the writing, and perhaps its essential unshareability, as though access to meaning is intentionally gated by language that resolutely excludes much subjectivity. Prynne's absent-body poetry is much admired for its depersonalised methodology by the underground, as Larkin's backward expression remains a constant resource to poets who reverse out of the present into a sometime English past, stuck like chewing gum to the 1950s, when most men looked middle-aged, styleless and frozen out of modernism, and waiting to be rained on by pre-Viagra impotence.

The publication in the same year of Louis Zukofsky's *A 22-23* as the finale to his language-crunching epic *A*, although the book's printing was unfavourably received by its author, was for Asa the achievement of publishing someone he looked up to as a role model in linguistically navigable poetry. Asa had spoken for years of his enthusiasm to publish Zukofsky, and in many ways, although he fulfilled his obligation to publish

Barry MacSweeney's *Odes* and Brian Marley's *Springtime in the Rockies* the following year, Zukofsky was the end of time moment for Trigram; the book suffering poor sales, critical neglect, with the bulk of the edition left undistributed in brown paper packets.

Falling as it did in punk Barry MacSweeney's *Odes* triggered a socially dissident and subversive thrust to the Trigram quota. The origins of the book dated back to the publication of MacSweeney's *Six Odes* (1972), a sequence that captivated Asa by its use of sensual imagery derived in part from altered state substances, but the book was a painfully slow six years in the making, with Barry adding new work in progress, and collecting sequences previously published in booklet form only like *Just 22 and I Don't Mind Dying*, and *Far Cliff Babylon*, under the composite title *Odes*, as by far his strongest collection. Volatile, lippy, and full of the intransigent Northern attitude he projected to counterpoint a natural romanticism MacSweeney was showcased at his best. Constantly shooting his lyric expansion down, there's the persistent feeling throughout of Barry stamping hard on his own poetry so as not to betray his indigenous working class roots. Extraordinarily gifted and with a visionary facility MacSweeney's *Odes* crash stratospheric frontiers in the attempt to achieve four-dimensional reality through torching-up supercharged language as extraordinary event.

> 'and the warm weather is holding'
> > far back, whisky
> nailed the plate, he
> kissed an Ace
> > On into
> overmuch, pukey niblets
> in the shadow of the magic mushroom
> children held room for grief in the mild autumn

Even when grounded in the ordinary Barry's imagery slashes awareness of his unusually gifted poetic chemistry; his criterion being, fuck off if you don't like it. At odds with most forms of British poetry MacSweeney navigated his own uncompromising brilliant pathway into self-destruct through chronic alcoholism; the disease that ruined and finally killed him in May 2000.

Dossier 3

Disclaimer: This is not a biography of Asa Benveniste and Trigram Press, but a personally selective mapping of significantly great aspects of both.

Excerpt from

The Glamour Poet versus Francis Bacon, Rent and Eyelinered Pussycat Dolls

(Shearsman Books, 2014)

Jeremy Reed

I sat there in fluffy blue topaz fog
with Asa Benveniste, spaghetti thin,
black shirted, moonstone ring, the kabala
mixed in his language, a word-soup
in which the alphabet swam like noodles
that steamed up into poetry;
Asa the maestro printer and poet
the eye that sanctioned Trigram Press,
there to fire gold in my teen poetry;
I was the poet he compared
to Rimbaud with my shook up imagery
and Jagger body, and his voice
pitched through blue toasted Camel smoke
was baritone cool like Leonard Cohen's
a generational '50s chilled out tone,
understated and lyrical,
a voice that unzipped women, it was silk
climbing like a morning glory
to poetry. We sat and crows convened
with their dodgy runic vocabulary
and threw black shapes, leather parabolas
through puffs of fog, the no-colour sky
like tonic drizzled into gin, the farm
a granite block in the valley
as unworked, off-limits intelligence
secured by a tax-fraudster drugs cartel.
Asa chain-smoked his soft-pack Lucky Strike
his language doing smoke signals,
nicotine semiotics, he wanted
a book from me, my formative
clotted implosions, hallucinated,
done for sensational imagery,
and I, already neural in my search
to kick poetry into sci-fi themes
wrote like dirty-bombing the dictionary
into my face, tattooed with words
stuck to me epidermally
like subjective iron crosses
that glittered with the tacky paste I wore

badged on my jacket in splashes
of ruby, green and nectarine.
Asa spoke of Trigram as poetry
subverting mainstream arteriosclerosis,
his travelled via Black Mountain
to New York fusion, pop and poetry,
Frank O'Hara and Bob Dylan jet-stream
free-associated, psychoactive
cocktail-shaken upended imagery,
magic, hoodoo and snake venom
appointed to the line, a stoned cowboy
appearing out the sun. We spoke of death
as Burroughs, the figure of death
as neural hologram, virtual junky,
an opiated infra-red
heroin-cuffed emissary, shoot death
into your veins like kerosene
into a plane, Bill put the skin on death
and a 3-piece Savile Row suit,
a Burlington Arcade cashmere jumper
in foggy blue or tin drum grey.
Asa collected detail like I do
and lived on a yoghurt a day,
Turkish coffee, Jack Daniels, J&B,
compact non-filter cigarettes
like Camel, Players, Lucky Strike, Pall Mall,
the field slowly emptied of mist
like a chilled bottle thawing, and more crows
appeared in primal diagrams
round a trio of colour-saturated oaks,
aggressive in their gutturals
as an Elizabethan madrigal…
We sat islanded by telepathy,
our juju register immediate,
our transfer like the speed of light,
my little completed by his sentences,
the sea up somewhere in the sky
as a jade puddle. He gave me his lemon book
The Atoz Formula, his language soaked

in printer's ink and occult imagery
like spooning gold dust from a jar
into imaginative chemistry.
Asa breathed language palpably
as smoke directed through his nostrils
under an antlered oak's twisted torso
the tree practising green yoga
rooted into one position
of photosynthesis. Asa spoke likes,
mostly Tom Raworth for his speed
and rushed synaptic imagery
like jewels shot through the veins
into adrenal energy
as coloured minerals. I count them up
my Asa letters, all black ink
as black as liquorice, I've 53
from London and Fakenham,
Leverton Street and Blue Tile House, letters
that came with books: our Jersey day
a white horse sipping at its blue shadow,
plane traffic rumbling in the sky,
the leather strap of Asa's black daybag
looped like a snake, our chosen site
this oak's green umbrella pitched at a sky
vibrating constantly with turbo
throttling back, deaccelerated roar
of skyways, and his lighter flame
snapped periodically into a surge
of orange-blue Benzedrine.
I read the *Atoz Formula* for weeks
instructed by its coded imagery
into a new poetic DNA,
a larynx shaping words by cellular
respiration, lowercase stems
and columnar blocks, the shapes
helically diagrammatic like sex,
showing me linguistic fuck,
the poem written like fellatio
orgasmic in its metric scale;

and Asa's *Poems of the Mouth*,
more like an oriental 69
in tricky metaphysics, deep throat stuff
worked in phoneme orbit, poetry
at work, a molecular thing
that got into me intravenously
from Asa's blue ophibian brushstrokes,
the poem erect like a cock or snake
and chartable by chakras
if you search their porous meridians.
Asa in London, Kentish Town,
a silver crew-neck, a Camel sighting
from obsidian ash tray,
his first scotch poured at 10.30am.
a twinkly amber Jack Daniels,
he'd got a manuscript from J.H. Prynne
a cool postmodern refrigerated
anti-narrative written at Ed Dorn's
no subject matter, just the thing
alien as an urinanalysis
with a sexy tone, a Prynne
semiotic abstraction, blue and red
if you see colours in a block
of chewing gum coloured poetry,
and Asa did in *News of Warring Clans*,
took it for tangential odd
and its impenetrable matte,
specific as a Toshiba accountant.

Asa Benveniste — Bibliography

compiled by Mitch Telfer

1966   *Poems of the Mouth* (Trigram)

1969   *The A to Z Formula* (Trigram)

1975   *Edge* (Joe Di Maggio)
       Listen (Doones)

1983   *Throw Out the Life Line Lay Out the Course* (Anvil)

1988   *Pommes Poems* (Arc)

1989   *Invisible Ink* (Singing Horse / Branch Redd)

JOINT PUBLICATIONS

1972   *Time Being* (with Tom Raworth & Ray DiPalma) (Blue Chair)

1975   *Dense Lens* (with Brian Marley) (Trigram)

BOOKLETS, BROADSIDES ETC.

1965   *The Spiral of the Mouth* (Trigram)

1967   *A Word in your Season* — Serigraphs (with Jack Hirschman)
                                                    (Trigram)

1968   *Free Semantic No. 2* (later version tipped into *For Bill Butler*)
                                        (Wallrich Books, 1970)

1969   *Count 3* (Cranium)

1972   *Umbrella* — New Year's Card (Wallrich Books)

1973   *It's the Same old Feeling Again* (Trigram)

1974   *Blockmaker's Black* (Broadside in box with Lyman Andrews,
       Lawrence Durrell, Ruth Fainlight, Sylvia Plath, Alan Sillitoe)
                                                    (Stream)
       Certainly Metaphysics — Broadside (Blue Chair)

1975   *Change* (Caligula)
       Cortege (n.p.)

1976   *A Part* (White Dog)

1977   *Loose Use* (Pig Press Hasty Edition)
       Colour Theory (Trigam)

1980   *Language Enemy Pursuit* (Poltroon)
       Amulet & High 8 — Poetry Cards (Trigram)

1989   *Textural* — Broadside (Turret)

1990   *Hadrian's Dream* (Circle)

Trigram Press Bibliography

compiled by Mitch Telfer

BOOKS

1965
Oswell Blakeston   *How To Make Your Own Confetti*

1966
George Andrews   *Burning Joy*
Asa Benveniste   *Poems of the Mouth*
Jack Hirschman   *Yod*
Anthology   *Residu 2*

1967
Piero Heliczer   *The Soap Opera*

1968
Anselm Hollo   *The Coherences*
Hugo Manning   *The Secret Sea*
Tom Raworth   *The Big Green Day*
John Esam / Hollo / Raworth   *Haiku*

1969
George Barker   *At Thurgarton Church*
Asa Benveniste   *The A to Z Formula*
Jim Dine   *Welcome Home Lovebirds*
Jack Hirschman   *Black Alephs*
David Meltzer   *Yesod*
Nathaniel Tarn   *October*
Lee Friedlander, Jim Dine   *Work from the Same House*
Anthology   *Dog, Running*

1970
Tom Raworth   *Lion Lion*

1971

Barry Cole — *Vanessa in the City*
Gavin Ewart — *Gavin Ewart Show*
David Wolton — *Fflipbook*
B.S. Johnson — *House Mother Normal*

1972

Paul Gogarty — *Snap Box*
Anselm Hollo — *Alembic*
B.S. Johnson — *Poems 2*
John Keys — *Hammersmith Poems*

1973

Asa Benveniste — *It's the Same Old Feeling Again*
Ivor Cutler — *Many Flies Have Feathers*
Tom Raworth — *Act*

1975

Asa Benveniste, Brian Marley — *Dense Lenz*
Gavin Ewart — *Be My Guest*
Tristan Tzara trs. Lee Harwood — *Selected Poems*
Jonathan Williams, Tom Phillips — *Imaginary Postcards*

1976

Abraham ben Samuel Abulafia — *The Path of Names*
Jeff Nuttall — *Objects*
Jeremy Reed — *The Isthmus of Samuel Greenberg*

1977

Ivor Cutler : — *A Flat Man*
J.H. Prynne — *News of Warring Clans*
Louis Zukofsky — *"A" 22 & 23*

1978

Barry MacSweeney — *Odes*
Brian Marley — *Springtime in the Rockies*

1980

Agneta Falk — *Here By Choice*

1981
Anthology
(Glen Baxter, Ian Breakwell,
Anthony Earnshaw, Asa Benveniste,
Ivor Cutler, Jeff Nuttall   *5 x 5*

ALSO

1972

Roberta Berke   *Sphere of Light*
                              (Joint publication with Fire)

BROADSIDES ETC.

1967

Jack Hirschman   *Jerusalem Ltd.*
Asa Benveniste, Jack Hirschman *A Word in Your Season*
Christopher Logue   *Some Contemporary Shit*
Various Signatories   *Backing for US Policies in Vietnam*

1968

Lionel Kearns   *The Birth of God*
Asa Benveniste   *Free Semantic No. 2*
                              Reprinted in smaller format as a tipped-
                              in broadside with *For Bill Butler*
                              (Wallrich Books 1970)

1973

David Meltzer   *What do I know of Journey*
Asa Benveniste   *It's the Same Old Feeling Again*

1977

Marc Vaux, Asa Benveniste   *Colour Theory*
Kevin Power, Ian Tyson   *Work in Progress*

Printed in July 2021
by Rotomail Italia S.p.A., Vignate (MI) - Italy